HAUNTED
HISTORY
OF
PHILADELPHIA

HAUNTED HISTORY
OF
PHILADELPHIA

JOSH HITCHENS

Haunted
America

Published by Haunted America
A Division of The History Press
Charleston, SC
www.historypress.com

All photos by the author unless otherwise noted.

First published 2022

Manufactured in the United States

ISBN 9781467151580

Library of Congress Control Number: 2022937927

Notice: The information in this book is true and complete to the best of our knowledge. It is offered without guarantee on the part of the author or The History Press. The author and The History Press disclaim all liability in connection with the use of this book.

This book is dedicated to all the "Creepers in Capes," the incredible storytellers who have been my work colleagues and friends at the Ghost Tour of Philadelphia for fifteen years as of this writing. My life is richer for having known all of you, and this book would not exist without your knowledge and expertise. You've all made me a better storyteller, whether you know it or not.

AND

In loving memory of Tim Reeser, author and cofounder of the Ghost Tour of Philadelphia, December 26, 1953–January 28, 2022.

AND

For Olive, when you are old enough.

CONTENTS

Acknowledgements

No one writes a book alone, and I have many people to thank for making the volume you hold in your hands a reality. First and foremost are J. Banks Smither and Zoe Ames, my editors at The History Press, who guided me through this process with consummate skill and support.

I am also immensely grateful for the assistance of many people and organizations who took the time to speak with me during the writing of this book, providing invaluable historical background and, in many cases, their own personal stories, some anonymously. I would particularly like to thank Kayla Anthony, Judy Smith and Mackenzie Warren of the Philadelphia Society for the Preservation of Landmarks; Jonathan Burton; Rachel Diamond (who first encouraged me to write about Mary Lum Girard for an episode of her excellent podcast *We're All Mad Here*); Mickey Herr; Eileen Reeser; and the Temple University Urban Archives.

I give special thanks to Megan Edelman and Thomas H. Keels, both of whom read early versions of this manuscript and gave me invaluable feedback. Mr. Keels is the author of seven wonderful books about Philadelphia history. Read them all. I also thank my partner, Dr. Jacob Glickman. Without his love and support, the book you hold in your hands would never have been written.

Finally, I would not be who I am, and I would not be writing this book, without the great joy of being a storyteller for the Ghost Tour of Philadelphia since 2007. If you live in Philadelphia or find yourself there on a visit and want to explore the darker side of its incredible history, go to www.ghosttour.com and buy a ticket. You will find yourself on a journey with an excellent storyteller wearing a cape and carrying a lantern to lead you through these shadowy cobblestoned streets at night. It might even be me. No matter which guide you get, we promise to tell you the truth, all the history and all about the many restless phantoms that still walk in this old City of Brotherly Love after dark.

Ghost stories are about how we face, or fail to face, the past—how we process information, how we narrate the past, and how we make sense of the gaps in that history.

—*Colin Dickey,* Ghostland: An American History in Haunted Places

————◦————

The challenge for historians when it comes to hauntings is not to separate fact from fiction, but to know when a folktale will illustrate some historical significance.

—Haunted History, *The History Channel, October 29, 1999*

————◦————

And thou, Philadelphia, the virgin settlement of this province—named before thou wert born—what love, what care, what service and what travail there have been to bring thee forth and to preserve thee from such as would abuse and defile thee. Oh, that thou mayest be kept from the evil that would overwhelm thee; that faithful to the God of thy Mercies, in the life of righteousness, thou mayest be preserved to the end.

—*"William Penn's Prayer for Philadelphia," 1684*

The Darker Side
of Philadelphia

I think I have a right to call myself a Philadelphian,
though I am not sure if Philadelphia is of the same opinion.

Those words begin the 1914 book *Our Philadelphia*, written by Elizabeth Robins Pennell, a journalist and author who was born and raised in Philadelphia but spent most of her adult life in England. I identify with her statement deeply. I was born and spent the first eighteen years of my life in Sussex County, Delaware, then moved to Philadelphia to attend college at Arcadia University (which itself is very haunted, as you will learn later). I fell head over heels in love with this richly historic, strange, miraculous, endlessly fascinating city, and I never left. As of this writing, I have lived in Philadelphia for over half of my life, nearly twenty years, but I am always conscious that compared to those who were born and raised in this extraordinary and uniquely American place, I am still a humble visitor.

My name is Josh Hitchens, and I tell ghost stories for a living. In the introduction to my first book published by The History Press, *Haunted History of Delaware*, I go into detail about how my passion for history and ghost stories began. There are countless connections between Philadelphia and the state of Delaware in the historical record; their shared destinies are, in many ways, inextricably intertwined. Since my grandparents took me on my first ghost tour in Colonial Williamsburg when I was eight years old, I knew what I wanted to do when I grew up, and here we are. In 2007, when I graduated from Arcadia University, the first job I applied for was to be a storyteller for

Statue of Chief
Tamanend at Penn's
Landing.

the Ghost Tour of Philadelphia, which is one of the oldest ghost tours in the
United States. The organization was established in 1995 by Eileen and Tim
Reeser, and you can see the preeminence of this organization in its website
address, which is www.ghosttour.com.

I will continue telling the ghost stories of Philadelphia as long as this city
is my home. Over the many years I have walked the dark corners of the
city's most historic places all alone, I have felt the strong presence of spirits
from the past. I have seen lights go on and off in the windows of buildings
I know are vacant of human habitation. I have stood inside the darkened
rooms of old houses and felt eyes looking at me when no one else is there.
Aside from the Ghost Tour of Philadelphia, I have worked in many of the
city's museums and historic sites over the years and experienced things that
cannot be explained by natural means, all of which are featured within
these pages.

I take great pride in saying at the beginning of my ghost tour in
Philadelphia, "I am not a paranormal investigator. I am a storyteller." I
believe there is a great power in that, of knowing that you are part of a chain
that goes back through the ages, ever since we learned to talk and sit around
a fire, telling stories to one another in the dark. And ghost stories are always
the best. When you feel truly afraid, you know you are alive. That moment
when you were truly, deeply frightened can burn itself into your memory
forever. Years later, you can recall every sensory detail, and you get the chill
again, and you shiver.

That is what a ghost story can do, if the telling is good. The receiving and
passing on of ghost stories and legends is, to me, the best and most enjoyable
gateway into discovering the hidden riches of local history, no matter where
you live.

THE HISTORY OF PHILADELPHIA does not begin with William Penn in 1682, as most books and tour guides would have you believe. It begins thousands of years earlier, when the land we now call Pennsylvania was home to the Lenni Lenape Native American people. Their territory also included what are now known as the states of Delaware, New Jersey and New York. Shelley DePaul, the administrative and education chief for the Lenape Nation of Pennsylvania, was interviewed about the history of her people in the first episode of the excellent thirteen-part historical documentary series *Philadelphia: The Great Experiment*, which you can watch for free on YouTube courtesy of History Making Productions:

> *The Lenape are the original people on this land. Archaeological evidence has proven that they've been here for thirteen thousand years. The river was the lifeblood of the land. It's sacred to our people. In our society, the women were the ones to make the important decisions. They were the ones to appoint the chiefs. Women were the holders of all property. It was very important to them to maintain a balance. They were very much aware of balance in all nature. The other tribes defined strength by forming this huge confederacy. The Lenape were not interested in doing that. They were not a warlike tribe. Their strength was their peacefulness. But they were certainly fierce enough warriors when they had to be.*

Nanticoke Lenni-Lenape Tribal Nation historian the Reverend John Norwood said, "Our people were numerous at one point. Early explorers talk about the campfires being so plentiful they lit the sky, even when they were still approaching the shoreline." The first European settlers began to arrive in 1609, first the Dutch, followed in 1638 by the Swedes, who created the colony of New Sweden. Philadelphia still honors its Swedish roots with the blue and yellow colors of its flag. The European colonists also brought with them infectious and deadly diseases such as smallpox, influenza and malaria, all of which devastated the Lenni Lenape population of the region. Norwood says,

> *A chief told a missionary that "for every one of you that arrives on a boat, ten of us die." There are stories of there not even being enough people left in villages to bury the dead. Some of the diseases attacked the oldest and the youngest. So, the ones who were the keepers of the wisdom and the ones who had the strength to perpetuate the communities were being wiped out.*

Historians estimate that European diseases killed approximately seventy-five percent of the region's Native American population.

By 1674, the British had taken control of the land formerly occupied by the Dutch and the Swedes. In 1681, King Charles II gave a huge tract of North American land to William Penn in order to pay back debts the king owed Penn's father. In England, William had faced persecution for his religious beliefs; he belonged to the Society of Friends, known pejoratively as Quakers. When he traveled to the New World to what would become known as Pennsylvania in 1682, William Penn formed a peace treaty with the Lenni Lenape people, meeting with Tamanend, the "Chief of Chiefs." Tamanend is reported to have said the Lenni Lenape and the English colonists would "live in peace as long as the waters run in the rivers and creeks and as long as the stars and moon endure." The location of their meeting is now preserved as Penn Treaty Park.

Unfortunately, this truce did not last forever. In 1737, over one million acres of land occupied by the Lenni Lenape for many thousands of years was stolen from them in a fraudulent exercise known as the Walking Purchase that was conducted by the sons of William Penn, who used forged documents and other trickery to cheat the tribes out of what rightfully belonged to them.

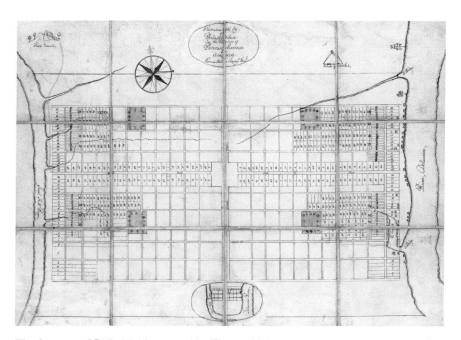

The first map of Philadelphia, created by Thomas Holme in 1683. *Public domain.*

In 2004, the Lenni Lenape sued the State of Pennsylvania to retrieve their ancestral territory. The case was dismissed, and the Supreme Court refused to take it up. Their land, which includes Philadelphia, remains stolen.

In letters, William Penn wrote that he intended the city of Philadelphia to be a "holy experiment," "the seed of a nation," where people of all kinds could live freely together without fear of persecution, a "green country town" that would be unlike any other city in the world. As a contrast with the confusingly winding streets of London, he laid out Philadelphia on a grid pattern, the model of which was still being followed centuries later. Because Penn had lived through the nightmare of the Great Fire of London in 1666, he also decreed that buildings be constructed of brick or stone, not wood, and placed five large squares of open land to make it more difficult for a catastrophic fire to occur. Unlike the brutal justice system of England, which favored the death penalty, Penn envisioned a system that was fairer and less harsh. Initially, the city of Philadelphia operated much as William Penn had intended, but the purity of its mission could not last forever. "Philadelphia, more than other American cities, has always struggled with its split personality," says author Thomas H. Keels in his book *Wicked Philadelphia*. Jennifer L. Green also writes of this unique duality in her book *Dark History of Penn's Woods*:

> *Beneath the golden mantle of utopia, however, seethed an underbelly of dissent, frustration, and violence. As early as 1693, the Provincial Council complained that Pennsylvanians were already violating Penn's proclamations against "Sabbath breaking, drunkenness, idleness, unlawful gaming, and all manner of prophanesse* [sic]*." The looseness of the laws of Pennsylvania seemed to encourage settlers to break them even more frequently. In hindsight, we can understand why diverse groups of immigrants from Germany, Ireland, Scotland, and elsewhere might not want to embrace the Quaker strictures against gambling, dancing, fancy dress, and theater. Staidness is not everyone's cup of tea.*

From its stolen inception, there have been strange shadows underneath Philadelphia's story that have almost never found their way into the official history books. On the one hand, there is the accepted narrative of the Founding Fathers and Mothers of the nation and their great works, but on the other hand, there is a much darker side to the City of Brotherly Love that has rarely been given a voice. That is why I wrote this book.

WILLIAM PENN HIMSELF PRESIDED over the first and only witchcraft trial to occur in Pennsylvania, although witchcraft was not legally a crime until 1718. But in 1683, in what is now known as Chester County, two women were accused of being witches. Like many women in Europe before them and in Salem, Massachusetts, after them, these two were branded as outsiders by their neighbors. Both women were older, and neither one of them spoke English. Margaret Mattson and Yeshro (some sources say Gethro) Hendrickson, both immigrants from Sweden, were accused of bewitching their neighbors' cows to stop them from giving milk, killing other livestock and appearing at night in spectral form, threatening their victims with a large knife. Two of Mattson's accusers were her daughter and son-in-law, who may have been interested in acquiring the substantial Ridley Creek farmland she owned. Eager to not follow Europe's example in executing scores of women who were accused of witchcraft with flimsy evidence, William Penn went to great lengths to ensure a fair trial. He allowed Margaret Mattson to defend herself, which was highly unusual in the seventeenth century. He hired a court interpreter as well, to overcome the language barrier. Penn himself asked questions of Margaret Mattson and the witnesses who had accused her in front of a twelve-man jury. The court records that we have left today suggest that Yeshro Hendrickson was perhaps not present at the trial, as no testimony attributed to her is mentioned.

Margaret Mattson denied all charges against her, saying, "These witnesses speak only by hearsay....I deny these accusations at my soul....Where is my daughter? Let her come and say so." There is one anecdote about this trial, handed down by folklore, that is not found in the scarce records that survive. Legend says that William Penn asked Margaret Mattson if she had ever flown through the air on a broomstick, as her accusers alleged. Mattson, perhaps due to a mistake by the interpreter, said, "Yes." The court erupted in gasps. William Penn considered this for a long moment, then said, correctly, that there was no law on the books preventing people from riding on broomsticks.

Finally, the jury reached its verdict. Margaret Mattson and Yeshro Hendrickson were found "guilty of having the common fame of a witch, but not guilty in the manner and form...indicted." In other words, the women were guilty of being *thought* to be witches but were not truly witches. They were ordered to pay a fine and sent back to their respective homes. The women and men accused of witchcraft in Salem, Massachusetts, in 1692, only nine years later, would not be fortunate enough to have a judge like William Penn.

Another famous Philadelphian that historical records show may have been a witch might surprise you: Betsy Ross, born Elizabeth Griscom in 1752 and glorified in American legend as the woman who sewed the first Stars and Stripes for George Washington. It is almost certain she did not, but the real Betsy Ross is well worth celebrating as an independent woman who persevered and ran a successful business based entirely on her own talent and skill despite immense obstacles, including being widowed thrice. One of Betsy's descendants, Lee Griscom, wrote in a 1945 letter: "It is said she had the gift of healing which she exercised secretly for fear of gaining the reputation of being a witch. She also had a remarkable gift for foreseeing events." In her definitive biography, *Betsy Ross and the Making of America*, author Marla R. Miller relates another supernatural incident passed down through time:

> *If the affidavits are to be believed, Ross planted the seeds of her own mythology in the 1820's and '30s as she regaled her children and grandchildren with stories of her youth, her work and life in Revolutionary Philadelphia….She laughed as she recounted a dream she had had in her youth…in which she saw "the letters GRAC in looking through a handkerchief toward the sky." Her friends had teased her that she was missing the e to spell grace, "but she replied that she had that in her first name, Elizabeth," and then happily explained to her listeners the vision's true meaning, how she couldn't have known then what she would in time, that "these letters were the initials of her various names after her three marriages": Elizabeth Griscom Ross Ashburn Claypoole.*

Today, the Betsy Ross House is one of the most popular tourist destinations in Philadelphia, although it is uncertain if Ross ever actually lived in that particular house. The bones of Betsy and her third husband, John Claypoole, were reinterred there in 1975 from Mount Moriah Cemetery in West Philadelphia, although whether the remains are truly those of Betsy and John is also somewhat controversial. An article from the Associated Press reported:

> *When anthropologist Dr. Allan Mann and two gravediggers excavated the site under the headstone where Mrs. Ross was supposed to be buried, they found nothing. They finally discovered a decayed coffin several feet away from where Mrs. Ross was supposed to have been. Through the caved-in lid, they spotted bones. Mann cautioned that although he will probably be able to tell if the skeleton was a woman, he may not be able*

A re-creation of Betsy's bedroom at the Betsy Ross House, where her ghost has reportedly been seen.

to tell if it was Betsy Ross or one of the two women, her daughter and granddaughter, records say were buried nearby. Mann, hired by the Betsy Ross Foundation to oversee the project, cautioned that whatever happened to Betsy Ross' remains may never be known for certain. The high acid content of the soil in the cemetery could mean that nothing is left of any bones, he suggested. A coffin buried in 1856 would not now be whole unless it were made of a wood like mahogany. Details of the move of the remains [to Mount Moriah Cemetery] *in 1856 are scarce and Mann suggested it is possible that the persons hired to do the job put only an empty casket in the ground or buried a dog. Anthropologists say it is common to find animal bones in old human graves.*

Nevertheless, bones attributed to Betsy Ross and John Claypoole are buried in the courtyard of what is now called the Betsy Ross House. Many visitors to the Betsy Ross House over the years have reported seeing her ghost on the property in what is said to have been her bedroom, kneeling by the bed as if in prayer or deep sorrow. In the basement of the house, staff and visitors have heard a woman's voice saying, "Pardon me, pardon me," when there is nobody there to pardon.

WISSAHICKON VALLEY PARK IS one of the treasures of Philadelphia, a perfect place to spend an afternoon forgetting the city around you. While exploring the largely unspoiled woods of the Wissahickon, it is easy to believe you are in another time. But there is also a spooky side to this beautiful place. The Wissahickon was the home of the first doomsday cult in North America, led by a Transylvanian mystic named Johannes Kelpius. Arriving in Philadelphia in 1684 with approximately forty followers, Kelpius and his "monks" traveled to Germantown and constructed a monastery in the woodland near what is now known as Hermit Lane. They called themselves the Society of the Woman of the Wilderness.

Inspired by a verse in the Book of Revelation, Kelpius believed the world would end in 1694. He and his followers used astronomy to map the stars, sometimes sheltering in man-made caves along the Wissahickon. When the world did not end in 1694, Johannes Kelpius revised his prediction to 1700. The world continued, and the group of hermits stayed where they were, faithful to their leader. They celebrated the sacred night of St. John's Eve, June 23, the date they arrived in Philadelphia, every year with a large bonfire in the forest and offerings to God. During one of these rituals, an observer recorded an extraordinary event. They saw arising from their fire "a white, obscure moving body in the air, which, as it approached, assumed the form and mien of an angel....It receded into the shadows of the forest and appeared again immediately before them as the fairest of the lovely."

Some believed that Johannes Kelpius was in possession of the fabled Philosopher's Stone, which gave its owner the power of alchemy (turning any base metal into gold) and also granted its owner the gift of eternal life. Kelpius is said to have kept the stone in a box that he called the Arcanum. Germantown native and author Joe Tyson, in an excellent historical article for Southern Cross Review called "The Monks of the Ridge," describes the end of the life of Johannes Kelpius, who would die of pneumonia at the relatively young age of thirty-five:

> According to Lutheran minister Henry Melchior Muhlenberg, the mystic believed that "he would not die a natural death but be transfigured...into the spiritual world." However, as death neared, [Kelpius] disabused himself of this illusion and told disciple Daniel Giessler: "I have received my answer. It is that dust I am and to dust I shall return. It is ordained that I shall die like all children of Adam." Kelpius then began putting his affairs in order. He handed Giessler a small box containing magical artifacts and instructed him to throw it into the Schuylkill River. Giessler set out on a mile hike to the Schuylkill but decided to hide the chest somewhere along the way. When he returned, Kelpius slowly sat up and fixed him with a stern gaze, saying: "Daniel, thou hast not done as I bid thee, nor

hast thou cast the casket into the river, but hast hidden it near the shore." The startled Giessler, "without even stammering an excuse, hurried to the river…and threw the casket into the water." As soon as he did so "the Arcanum exploded…and out of the water came flashes of lightning and peals like unto thunder." Some believe that the Philosopher's Stone still lies in the depths of the Schuylkill, close to Wissahickon Creek.

The "Cave of Kelpius" as it appeared in 2012. *Photo by Steven L. Johnson. Wikimedia Commons.*

The monks buried the body of Johannes Kelpius near the creek. With their leader gone, the last hermits of the Wissahickon slowly dwindled until only six of the faithful remained. To this day, the ghostly specters of six monks in brown robes are sometimes seen walking along the Wissahickon's Forbidden Drive when the moon is full. One of the "caves" built by the monks still survives and can be found on Hermit Lane. It is still used by individuals as a site for occult rituals from time to time. When I last visited the "Cave of Kelpius" in 2020, there were melted red candles, as well as animal bones and feathers, inside of it.

YOU CANNOT SPEAK ABOUT the haunted history of Philadelphia without touching on the Yellow Fever Epidemic of 1793, one of the most horrific times the city has ever known. Between August 1 and November 9 of that year, five thousand citizens of Philadelphia were killed by this disease, accounting for 10 percent of the city's total population. Between October 7 and 13 alone, 711 Philadelphians died from the yellow fever. The entire government, along with 20,000 other residents, fled the city. The streets were eerily empty and quiet. Horse-drawn carriages called "death carts" roamed the city to collect the infected dead, most of whom were buried in mass graves. Dr. Benjamin Rush, a signer of the Declaration of Independence, stayed in Philadelphia trying to treat the fever, the cause of which was then unknown. J.H. Powell writes of this terrifying summer in his definitive history *Bring Out Your Dead*:

By the end of the first week, the fever was grimly advertising itself. Scenes which reminded Rush of his histories of true plagues began to confront him as he moved through the streets. In homes through the settled part of town, persons of all ages were being stricken. Lassitude, glazed eyes, chills, fevers, headaches, nausea, retching, and nosebleeds would suddenly attack people in the best of health. These symptoms, more violent than any of the doctors had ever observed, would be followed by a yellow tinge of the eyeballs, puking, fearful straining of the stomach, the black vomit, hiccoughs, depression, "deep and distressed sighing, comatose delirium," stupor, purplish discolorations of the whole body, finally death. It was quick and desperately severe. In one case it killed in twelve hours, though it usually reached its crises in four days.

Dr. Rush also noticed the disease was accompanied by itchy red eruptions in the skin that "resembled mosquito bites." Although it was not discovered during the epidemic of 1793, what Dr. Rush observed was correct. Yellow fever is transmitted to human beings by mosquitos, which were (and are) abundant in Philadelphia during the warmer months. The death toll of this epidemic changed the city forever and effectively ended the possibility of it becoming the permanent capital of the United States. With so many people dying in such a short amount of time, it is no surprise that the yellow fever epidemic created several ghosts who still linger today.

George Lippard made Philly's Jekyll and Hyde nature the explosive primary subject of his 1845 Gothic novel *The Quaker City, or the Monks of Monk Hall*, which became the best-selling book the United States had ever seen at the time, only to be eclipsed by Harriet Beecher Stowe's *Uncle Tom's Cabin* seven years later. Lippard's *The Quaker City* was inspired by a real, horrific murder case that occurred in 1843—the murder of Mahlon Hutchinson Heberton, committed by Singleton Mercer. It was alleged that Heberton led Mercer's sixteen-year-old sister Sarah to a brothel and assaulted her at gunpoint. Just days after this, Singleton Mercer shot Mahlon Heberton dead as vengeance for his sister's violated honor and pain. After a sensational trial, during which Sarah Mercer provided harrowing testimony about her assault, her brother Singleton Mercer was found not guilty by reason of insanity.

The Quaker City's lurid exposé of the dark and secret vices indulged by members of Philadelphia's high society caused significant controversy at the time of its publication. After a theatrical version of *The Quaker City* was announced, to be performed at the Chestnut Street Theater, the show was canceled due to the threat of riots. As deliciously grotesque as the book is, its events and characters were based on truths and clearly touched a nerve with the people it was intended to indict. One of the novel's most incisive passages is this:

Philadelphia is not so pure as it looks....Alas, alas, that I should have to say it....Whenever I behold its regular streets and formal look, I think of The Whited Sepulcher, without [on the outside] *all purity, within, all rottenness and dead men's bones.*

Cover page image of *The Quaker City, or The Monks of Monk Hall* (1845) by George Lippard. *Art by Felix Octavius Carr Darley. Public domain.*

Elizabeth Robins Pennell, whom I quoted at the beginning of this introduction to the *Haunted History of Philadelphia*, was also the first person to write about the specters experienced in the City of Brotherly Love. She had a regular weekly column in the *Philadelphia Press* newspaper, which on January 1884 was titled: "Our Own Ghosts." In this article, she related several local ghost stories she had collected from contemporary residents of haunted places in the city. The response to Elizabeth Robins Pennell's first article on Philly's phantoms was immense, so much so that she published a follow-up article with more terrifying tales of ghosts in Philadelphia. She wrote, "That Philadelphia, a city so noted for its aristocracy and its old houses, should have ghost stories, is a matter of course."

I COULD NOT AGREE more. The ghost stories of Philadelphia could fill many volumes, but I have collected my favorites in this book. This is the city where Edgar Allan Poe lived and where he began to write some of his most immortal works, including "The Black Cat" and "The Raven," the inspiration for which, some say, was Charles Dickens's pet raven Grip, still lovingly preserved in the rare books room at the Free Library of Philadelphia. This is the city visited by author Bram Stoker as he wrote his immortal novel *Dracula*; his research notes are now on display in the extraordinary collection of the Rosenbach Museum and Library. This is the city where notorious serial killer H.H. Holmes was finally caught and executed in 1896 in a South Philadelphia prison. The prison has since been demolished, and the land where it stood is currently the parking lot of an ACME supermarket.

And now, as I have done for over fifteen years, let me take you on a tour of this city of restless spirits. We'll begin in the historic district of Old City and then move further out to other chilling sites where the dead are not quiet.

Several years ago, a man approached me at the end of my Ghost Tour of Philadelphia one night. He said, "I'm a psychic. I want to tell you that they all know who you are, and they are very interested in what you're doing." I took that in for a long moment, and then I replied to him, "I know." Telling the stories of these human beings, many of whom would be forgotten otherwise if it weren't for the tales of their hauntings, is an almost holy calling for me. I want them all to be remembered, and every time, I hope to tell their stories well and true, as I do here.

Come join me on a journey through the darker side of Philadelphia's history.

If you dare…

CHAPTER 1

A CREEPY CRIME IN CARPENTER'S HALL

As you walk down Chestnut Street toward Fourth Street in Old City, Philadelphia, your eyes may be drawn to a remarkable building that stands at the end of long and narrow cobblestone path. If you venture down that path, you will come face-to-face with a brick structure of impeccable and stately Georgian architecture. During the day, its doors are open for tours, but at night it is locked up tight, and the building is eerily illuminated by lights, in sharp contrast to the surrounding darkness. This is Carpenter's Hall, one of the most significant and at the same time one of the most unsung buildings from the early history of Philadelphia. Here is where the First Continental Congress began to meet in 1774 before eventually moving to the Pennsylvania State House a few blocks away. Carpenter's Hall is also the site of the first recorded bank robbery in the history of the United States. Out of that crime, a gruesome ghost story was born.

The Carpenter's Company of the City and County of Philadelphia was founded in 1724, its first members arriving in Philadelphia alongside William Penn. They were and still are today master builders, experts in the crafts of architectural design and engineering, dedicated to a standard of excellence that has remained undiminished for nearly three hundred years. Many of the most notable buildings constructed in colonial Philadelphia were the work of Carpenter's Company members, and their expertise continues to be felt in contemporary Philadelphia with their construction of skyscrapers and stadiums. Since its founding in 1724, the company has had a little over nine hundred members. If you visit Carpenter's Hall today, you can see handwritten lists of them all.

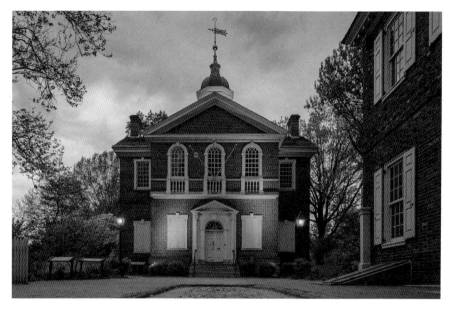

Carpenter's Hall in 2015. Photo by Pbjamesphoto. *Wikimedia Commons.*

In 1768, the Carpenter's Company purchased a plot of land on Chestnut Street, and the construction of Carpenter's Hall, designed by member Robert Smith, began on February 5, 1770. In January 1771, the company held their first meeting in the building, although it would not be fully completed until 1774. The impeccable design of Carpenter's Hall, with its many spacious rooms, almost immediately attracted the eye of other organizations that wished to rent the space. In 1773, the Library Company of Philadelphia, established by Benjamin Franklin, occupied the second floor. It was, in essence, the first public library in the United States. Reverend Manasseh Cutler said of this library in a letter, "Every modern author of any note, I am told, is to be met with here, and large additions are annually made."

By 1774, revolution was in the air after the Boston Tea Party, and Carpenter's Hall would be used for an even more momentous purpose. Because the nearby Pennsylvania State House was currently occupied, the delegates that would become the First Continental Congress decided to make Carpenter's Hall their first meeting place. As they convened in Philadelphia on September 5, 1774, John Adams wrote:

> *At ten, the delegates all met at the City Tavern, and walked to the Carpenter's Hall, where they took a view of the room, and of the chamber where there is*

an excellent library. There is also a long entry, where gentlemen may walk, and a convenient chamber opposite to the library. The general cry was, that this was a good room, and the question was put, whether we were satisfied with this room, and it passed in the affirmative.

During this First Continental Congress, all the colonies at last came together in the acknowledgement that something must be done about the tyrannical rule of England and the Crown, crafting the Declaration of Rights and Grievances. During October 1774 at Carpenter's Hall, Virginia delegate Patrick Henry made a speech that helped set the wheels in motion for the American Revolution: "The distinctions between Virginians, Pennsylvanians, New Yorkers, and New Englanders are no more. I am not a Virginian, but an American!"

That month, according to the official records, the delegates agreed to convene a Second Continental Congress in May 1775 "unless the redress of grievances…be obtained before that time." Of course, the King of England remained intractable toward the colonies, and Congress would meet again, this time at the Pennsylvania State House, which would later become known as Independence Hall.

In 1798, CARPENTER'S HALL was being used for yet another purpose as the home of the newly formed Bank of Pennsylvania. The bank vault was located in the hall's dark basement, protected by an iron gate. On August 11, 1798, a blacksmith named Patrick Lyon was hired by carpenter Samuel Robinson to make new locks for the bank vault. Lyon finished the job on August 13. He had worked in great haste, because in August 1798, the city of Philadelphia was in the midst of another yellow fever epidemic. Patrick Lyon had lost his wife, Ann, and their nine-month-old daughter Clementine to the disease in 1797, so he was eager to flee the city to save his life.

Patrick Lyon was not alone in his eagerness to leave Philadelphia. President John Adams had already left the capital city, and most of the United States government went with him. Although this epidemic was nowhere near as catastrophic as 1793, approximately 1,300 Philadelphians would die of the disease during the sweltering summer months of 1798. As Lyon prepared to leave Philadelphia with his nineteen-year-old assistant Jamie, he noticed Samuel Robinson and another man drinking in a tavern. He remembered both men having visited his blacksmith shop while work on the new bank vault locks was being done, and he felt uneasy. To Patrick Lyon, Robinson and the other man seemed to behave suspiciously: "They were up to no good," as he later wrote.

Lyon and his assistant Jamie booked passage on a ship to Cape Henlopen and arrived in the town of Lewes, Delaware, on August 28, 1798. Unfortunately, during the voyage, it became clear that young Jamie was sick with the dreaded yellow fever. Within two days of their arrival in Lewes, Jamie was dead.

As the end of August 1798 approached, Philadelphia had become a ghost town, the streets eerily deserted, the citizens who remained not daring to venture outside their homes for fear of the plague. The government had fled the city; law enforcement was in disarray. It was the perfect setting for an audacious crime to take place, the first of its kind in American history.

In the dark of night on August 31 or in the early morning hours of September 1, 1798, the Bank of Pennsylvania at Carpenter's Hall was robbed. The exact amount stolen was recorded in historical records: $162,821.61, which would be approximately three million dollars in today's money. There was no sign of forced entry—no broken doors or windows—and the new locks that Patrick Lyon had made for the bank vault were undamaged. To the authorities, this was, to put it in modern language, clearly an inside job.

The prime suspect in the robbery was, of course, Patrick Lyon, who had made the locks and the keys that opened them. And, after all, hadn't he fled Philadelphia around the time this heinous crime was committed? It seemed to be an open-and-shut case, and the police immediately began searching for Lyon throughout Philadelphia and nearby New Jersey.

Word of the bank robbery at Carpenter's Hall reached Patrick Lyon all the way down in Lewes, Delaware. Eager to clear his name, he booked passage on a ship home, but the ship would only go as far as the city of Wilmington, Delaware, since Philadelphia was still infested with the terror of yellow fever. So Patrick Lyon walked from Wilmington all the way to a Philadelphia police station, where he announced that he had come 150 miles to surrender himself and prove his innocence. He related the story of the strange man who had watched him make the locks and behaved suspiciously at the tavern, saying that this unknown man, who had been seen with Samuel Robinson, was the likely culprit. The authorities did not believe Patrick Lyon's story. They placed Lyon under arrest and threw him into the notorious Walnut Street Jail.

Meanwhile, the "strange man" Lyon had mentioned began depositing large sums of money at various Philadelphia banks, including the Bank of Pennsylvania at Carpenter's Hall, which he had recently robbed. His name was Isaac Davis, a member of the Carpenter's Company. Police arrested him, and Davis quickly confessed that he and a night porter at Carpenter's Hall named Tom Cunningham were responsible for this inside job. Incredibly, the governor of Pennsylvania, in exchange for returning the stolen money and a full confession, pardoned Isaac Davis, who never spent a single hour in jail. What happened to Isaac Davis after this is unknown, but in the membership scrolls of the Carpenter's Company, his name is marked with an *X*, suggesting he was expelled from membership after evidence of his crime came to light.

Tom Cunningham, the man who let Isaac Davis into Carpenter's Hall, suffered a different kind of punishment. Cunningham slept in one of the small rooms that were rented out to lodgers in the attic of Carpenter's Hall. In the days following the robbery, those working at the bank began to notice a horrible smell in the building. When they searched Carpenter's Hall to find its source, they were led to Tom Cunningham's attic room. Opening the door, they encountered the horrific sight of Cunningham's decomposing corpse, covered in blood and bodily fluids. It seemed that the yellow fever epidemic of 1798 had claimed another victim. Or perhaps the truth is even more sinister. Some have suggested that Tom Cunningham may have been murdered by Isaac Davis after the robbery to ensure his silence. The condition of the body by the time it was discovered made it impossible for a cause of death to be accurately determined, and any corpse that may have even potentially been a victim of the fever was always disposed of quickly.

You would think that with a full confession from Isaac Davis and the death of his only accomplice, Tom Cunningham, Patrick Lyon would have been freed immediately. But this did not happen, and his bail was set impossibly high. The police were still convinced that Lyon must have had something to do with the bank robbery and refused to let him go, even after Isaac Davis explicitly put in writing that Lyon was totally innocent. Patrick Lyon later drily and bitterly wrote, "I found I was in the hands of those who are not the most intelligent of mankind."

In his bleak twelve-by-four-foot cell at the Walnut Street Jail, which he described as "cold, damp, unwholesome and solitary," Patrick Lyon suffered for months. Inside the walls of the jail, the yellow fever ravaged the population of prisoners. Lyon, too, caught the fever, but unlike his wife, daughter and assistant Jamie, he survived it. Finally, in January 1799, after three long months of imprisonment, a grand jury exonerated Patrick Lyon, and he was free to go.

Stairs to the second floor of Carpenter's Hall.

Immediately afterward, Patrick Lyon filed a civil lawsuit against the Bank of Pennsylvania for malicious prosecution and false imprisonment, and he won. His settlement came to $9,000—which would be approximately $250,576 today—a sum of money that allowed him to live in comfort for the rest of his life. In true American form, Patrick Lyon then wrote and published a tell-all memoir entitled *The Narrative of Patrick Lyon, Who Suffered Three Months Severe Imprisonment in Philadelphia Gaol, on Merely a Vague Suspicion of Being Concerned in the Robbery of the Bank of Pennsylvania: With His Remarks Thereon*. It sold extremely well.

Today, there is a portrait hanging in the Pennsylvania Academy of the Fine Arts in Philadelphia by artist John Neagle called *Pat Lyon at the Forge*. Commissioned by Lyon himself, the painting shows him standing nobly in his blacksmith attire at his anvil, with the cupola of the Walnut Street Jail in the background behind him.

EVER SINCE THE DECAYING body of Tom Cunningham was discovered in the attic in September 1798, Carpenter's Hall has been haunted. People walking up to the historic landmark have sometimes been disturbed by the sudden sound of footsteps walking right behind them. When they turn around to see who it is, there is no one there—no one they can see, anyway. People who work inside of Carpenter's Hall have also heard the sound of disembodied footsteps ascending the staircase that leads up to the second and third floors. The footsteps are always described as being very loud, as if made by someone wearing heavy boots, pacing back and forth. Whenever the footsteps are investigated, no explanation is ever found.

An especially vivid and unsettling account of the haunting of Carpenter's Hall was recorded by author Elizabeth P. Hoffman in her 1992 book *In Search of Ghosts: Haunted Places in the Delaware Valley*. For that book, Hoffman interviewed James and Hazelle O'Connor, who worked as the caretakers of Carpenter's Hall in 1960, living on the second floor of the building.

One night, around midnight, as James and Hazelle were settling into bed, they suddenly heard loud footsteps stomping around in the disused attic above their heads. Terrified that a burglar had broken in, they quietly called the police. As they waited for the officers to arrive, they huddled under their covers and listened as the footsteps in the attic became louder and louder. Finally, they heard two police officers arrive. Too frightened to leave their bedroom, James and Hazelle opened a window and threw the key to the front door down to the police. The police officers opened the front door and began to ascend the stairs to the attic to confront the intruder. At this time, James and Hazelle both noticed that the footsteps in the attic had stopped. They held their breath, waiting for whatever was about to happen next.

Then there was a knocking on their bedroom door that caused them to jump. They opened the bedroom door. One of the officers said, "Hey, everything is fine. There's nobody up there."

James O'Connor said, "What do you mean there's nobody up there? We both heard someone walking around for the past half hour."

The officers smiled at them, almost smirking. "Look, the floor's covered in dust. There are no footprints. No one was up there. Not for a long time by the look of it." And then they handed back the key to the front door. James and Hazelle both stood in shock, and then both led the officers down the stairs and to the front door of Carpenter's Hall.

Then one of the officers said, "Don't worry about it. We've had calls from other people who have lived here before about hearing footsteps, but there's never anybody there. One thing though, you've got a dead animal up there. The smell is awful. I guarantee you no one would want to walk around up there with a smell like that."

After the officers had gone, James and Hazelle, armed with flashlights, began to ascend the stairs to the attic. As they got to the attic door, the smell of decay was so overpowering that Hazelle almost became sick. She pulled her husband downstairs, saying they could take care of whatever it was the next morning.

Once the sun was up, both James and Hazelle felt a little foolish. Holding towels over their faces to help minimize the smell, they went up to the attic to take care of whatever poor animal had gotten trapped and died up there. But when they got up to the attic, the horrible smell was gone. The attic smelled like dust and old wood, nothing more.

A few nights later, a little after two o'clock in the morning, James and Hazelle were again awoken by the sound of heavy footsteps in the attic. It lasted for about twenty minutes, then stopped. James O'Connor opened their bedroom door, and again they were hit by the sickly sweet odor of death. The next morning, the smell was gone again. A week or so later, the same events repeated themselves. James and Hazelle turned the television on with the volume loud enough to mask the sound of the footsteps and were finally able to begin sleeping through the night.

However, the attic was not the only part of Carpenter's Hall where the O'Connors experienced paranormal activity. The basement, the former location of the vault of the Bank of Pennsylvania, is also haunted by an unnerving presence. The first indication of this occurred when James and Hazelle's son came to visit them on a break from college. He elected to sleep in the basement and took his sleeping bag downstairs to go to bed.

He did not stay down in the basement long. After less than thirty minutes, he came back up to the second floor, sleeping bag in tow. When his parents asked him what was wrong, he seemed shaken and said, "I don't know, but I felt like there was something watching me down there." He spent the night sleeping on the floor of his parents' room.

Not long after that, Hazelle O'Connor went down to the basement to do a load of laundry, accompanied by her dog. As Hazelle walked into the room toward the washer and dryer, a wooden chair fell over by itself. She stood staring at the overturned chair as her dog began to whimper. Hazelle thought to herself, "This is ridiculous, I need to do my laundry." She picked up the chair, put it down and set the overloaded laundry basket on top of it. As she was opening up the lid of the washing machine, the chair, with the laundry basket on it, fell over again, just as if someone had pushed it. Her dog began to growl at a dark corner of the basement, then started barking and ran up the stairs. Hazelle followed the dog and never did laundry in the basement alone again for the remainder of the time she and her husband lived there.

Subsequent caretakers and other workers at Carpenter's Hall have felt deeply uncomfortable in the basement. Several people over the years have reported seeing the dark, shadowy silhouette of a man in the basement when they have gone down there alone. Perhaps Tom Cunningham is still haunting the scene of his crime—and his mysterious, grisly death—over two hundred years later.

CARPENTER'S HALL IS NOT on the standard route of the Ghost Tour of Philadelphia, but it is one of several extra locations that guides are invited to visit if they choose. For many years, I have always begun my ghost tour with Carpenter's Hall, because I believe it is an essential historic site in American history that is too often overlooked by locals and tourists, and it shouldn't be.

One night, several years ago, a woman who had been on my tour with her two children came up to me at the end of it, and she said she had an experience she wanted to share with me. This is what she said to me, quietly and intensely, while her children were out of earshot:

> *You may not believe me, but this is what happened. I visited Carpenter's Hall earlier today with my kids. We were looking around at all the displays when all of a sudden there was this horrible smell in the room on the first floor. Just a minute or two later, the employees said they had to close the building and they were sorry, but they basically just shooed us all out of the building immediately and slammed the door shut in our faces, and I heard it lock. And I was really concerned, because the smell that was in the room was something I recognized. I'm a police officer, and I've unfortunately experienced it before. There's no other smell like it. It was the smell of a rotting human corpse.*

CHAPTER 2

THE BURNING BRIDE
OF THE CITY TAVERN

If you travel on Walnut Street toward Penn's Landing, you will be confronted with the majestic spectacle of the Merchant's Exchange building, with a sea of cobblestones behind it. Walking on the stone paths, you will come across a sign that reads: "City Tavern, established 1773." This was the birthplace of fine American cuisine and an important meeting place for all the movers and shakers of colonial Philadelphia. However, the City Tavern that currently stands is not the original building. The first City Tavern was partially destroyed by fire in 1834 and fully demolished twenty years later, in 1854. By then, the City Tavern was long past its golden age, so much so that the *Pennsylvania Gazette* wrote on the occasion of its demolition: "Nobody is going to miss this Tavern except those persons living in the past."

It is somewhat ironic that the City Tavern would eventually be reborn out of a passionate desire to restore the past, meticulously reconstructed on its original site in time for the bicentennial celebrations of 1976. Beginning in 1994, the tavern was reinvented again by world-renowned chef Walter Staib, who received the job after winning the approval of Congress. Chef Staib turned the City Tavern into a first-class restaurant, filling its menu with authentic and delicious eighteenth-century recipes made with the freshest and finest ingredients available. In addition to the food, the interior of the building was restored to what it would have looked like in its heyday, and all the staff who interacted with customers were dressed in period costume. To walk through the doors of the City Tavern was to take a step backward in time, enabling every diner to experience

The City Tavern today.

an incredible meal as if they might see Benjamin Franklin or George and Martha Washington enjoying a lavish feast at the next table.

Perhaps because the City Tavern's eighteenth-century atmosphere was so lovingly re-created, that is the reason why its resident spirits returned to the new building. For the City Tavern is haunted not by only one ghost. There are at least two ghosts who have been experienced by staff and visitors alike ever since its glorious resurrection in the twentieth century.

THE SAME *PENNSYLVANIA GAZETTE* that greeted the City Tavern's destruction in 1854 with such disdain and indifference sang a completely different tune soon after the tavern first opened its doors in December 1773. On February 17, 1774, the newspaper published this notice:

> *City Tavern, Philadelphia. Daniel Smith begs leave to inform the public, that the gentleman proprietors of the City Tavern have been pleased to approve of him, as a proper person to keep said tavern: in consequence of which he has completely furnished it, and, at a very great expense, has laid in every article of the first quality, perfectly in the style of a London tavern.....He has also fitted up a genteel coffee room, well attended, and properly supplied with English and American papers and magazines. He hopes his attention and willingness to oblige, together with the goodness of his wines and larder, will give the public entire satisfaction, and prove him not unworthy of the encouragement he has already experienced. The City Tavern in Philadelphia*

was erected at great expense, by a voluntary subscription of the principal gentlemen of the city, for the convenience of the public, and is by much the largest and most elegant house occupied in that way in America.

Philadelphia, which in 1773 was the largest city in North America and the second-largest city in the English-speaking world, immediately took the City Tavern to its heart. Although the food and drink served was of the highest quality to be found anywhere in Philadelphia, the tavern kept its prices reasonably low to accommodate as many patrons as possible. And almost at once, the City Tavern became the heartbeat of the town, the place to go to learn the latest news and gossip while enjoying meals with as many as twenty courses, which John Adams rhapsodically spoke of as being "as elegant as were ever laid on a table."

Indeed, the City Tavern had opened its doors at exactly the right time. When Paul Revere arrived in Philadelphia with the news that the English had closed the port in revenge for the Boston Tea Party, the City Tavern is where he went. As the delegates from the newly formed First Continental Congress arrived in Philadelphia in the fall of 1774, they visited the tavern before they went to their lodgings. Entering the city for the first time, even John Adams, as notoriously difficult to impress as he was, described the City Tavern as "the most genteel one in America." Every Saturday, many of the delegates would gather for a long meal at the tavern, no doubt discussing, off the record and over copious quantities of Madeira wine, the momentous events that were shaping the new nation-to-be.

When the American Revolution began in 1775, the City Tavern became a nerve center and unofficial headquarters for those who were involved in the war, including George Washington. Two years later, on July 4, 1777, the very first Independence Day celebration was held at the tavern "with festivity and ceremony becoming the occasion," as John Adams wrote. In 1778, the wildest party ever to be held at the tavern occurred. According to *The City Tavern Cookbook*:

A party of 270, including ambassadors and ministers from Spain and France, attended. The bill was £2,995—only £500 of that was for food. The rest was for a stupefying amount of alcohol, including 522 bottles of Madeira, 116 large bowls of punch, nine bottles of toddy, six bowls of sangria, twenty-four bottles of port, and two tubs of grog for artillery soldiers. Understandably, the party turned boisterous—the bill also covered ninety-six broken plates and glasses, as well as five decanters.

Overindulgence of alcohol was also the cause of the first tragedy that occurred at the City Tavern, one that left the building's first resident ghost in its wake. If you have the good fortune to peruse *The City Tavern Cookbook* by Walter Staib and Paul Bauer, amid the pages of over two hundred mouthwatering eighteenth-century recipes, you will find this unexpected note:

> *Modern-day City Tavern staff swear there's a ghost in the restaurant—table settings are moved, dishes come crashing off the wall. Who knows? Maybe it's the nameless waiter murdered in the original City Tavern by Col. Craig on January 3, 1783, after a drunken brawl. The murderer was never prosecuted, some say because of the class differences between the two men.*

This murder of an innocent waiter at the City Tavern is a matter of historical record, and although the story was hushed up and not reported by the newspapers at the time, it was written about in the journal of a man named Samuel Rowland Fisher:

> *This afternoon heard that one of the waiters or servants at the City Tavern had been run through with a sword and killed by an Officer. All these Officers now quartered in town had been invited by some of the citizens to dine at the City Tavern, and this murder has been said to have been done by one of them while drunk.*

Fisher added in his entry the following day: "Heard that the waiter at the City Tavern was killed by a man known by the appellation of Colonel —— Craig." News of this scandalous murder also reached a man named George Nelson, who recorded in his diary that the waiter had been stabbed in the chest by Colonel Craig's sword and bled to death within ten minutes. He also added that those who witnessed the murder were being pressured to stay silent. Another Philadelphian, Daniel Newton, also wrote, "I am informed that nothing is done or like to be done to —— Craig, on account of his killing the man at the City Tavern on the 3rd of this month."

The reluctance of all these men to suppress the first name of the colonel, even though they were disgusted by the way the murder was being covered up, is telling. It suggests that this was an important man, well connected, worth protecting from scandal that would affect the military. This is borne out by a passage in Joseph J. Kelley's book *Life and Times in Colonial Philadelphia*: "A drunken brawl involving American officers led to the murder of a waiter, and General Anthony Wayne shielded the suspect from the searching constabulary."

Although I cannot prove it, there is one Colonel Craig from this period in history that fits the bill as the culprit. This man commanded the Third Pennsylvania Infantry Regiment during the American Revolution from August 1, 1777, to January 1, 1783, two days before the drunken killing of the waiter at City Tavern. After the war was over, he was made a brigadier general. After retiring from the military, he became a judge and died in Allentown, Pennsylvania, in 1832 at the age of ninety-two years. His first name is an extremely common one. I'll just say that it begins with the letter *T* and ends with the letter *S*. I'll let you draw your own conclusions.

It is no wonder that the ghost of this waiter remains earthbound centuries after his untimely demise. His killer, due to his military rank and high social status, got away with murder. Perhaps that is why his spirit moves plates around, as well as tables and chairs, during the night, when the tavern should be empty. Perhaps that is why he causes dishes and glassware to fall to the floor and be broken, in deep rage at the loss of his life and the miscarriage of justice that followed it.

There have also been reports from various diners at the City Tavern over the past three decades of noticing one of the costumed waiters standing in one of the dining rooms very still, staring at them, not moving, not blinking. Then they watch as the waiter slowly puts his hand on his chest, and they watch as his white shirt begins to turn red with blood. Then the waiter collapses to the floor. When his body hits the floor, he vanishes, still waiting for the justice that will never come.

To celebrate the successful conclusion of the Constitutional Convention, the members of Congress went straight from Independence Hall to the City Tavern to celebrate the new Constitution of the United States of America. George Washington wrote on September 15, 1787:

> *The business being thus closed, the members adjourned to the City Tavern, dined together and took a cordial leave of each other; after which I returned to my lodgings, did some business and received the papers from the Secretary of the Convention, and retired to meditate on the momentous work which had been executed.*

In April 1789, the City Tavern hosted a grand banquet for George Washington as he passed through Philadelphia on his way to New York to be inaugurated as the first president of the United States. As always at the tavern, there was a seemingly limitless supply of libations to enjoy, and in true Philadelphia fashion, such a good time was had that the fifty-seven-year-old president-elect had to sleep at the City Tavern that night instead of continuing his journey as planned.

This seems to have been the last truly grand event that took place at the City Tavern, when its rooms were filled with the greatest of the great, the men and women who would enter the history books. By the early 1800s, the tavern still existed but had fallen out of fashion—so much so that when it was badly damaged by fire in 1834, there were few who mourned its closure.

However, that fire in 1834 is the catalyst that created the second ghost of the City Tavern.

It was on a day in March 1834 that a wedding was due to take place at the City Tavern. The names of the bride and groom have not been recorded by history, but the circumstances surrounding that day have been handed down through generations of Philadelphians. On that day, which some sources cite as March 22, 1834, the wedding party arrived at the City Tavern, making all the necessary preparations for this joyous event, the union of two people in love in holy matrimony.

As the story goes, the groom was feeling a bit nervous, so he and his friends decided to have a few drinks at the bar to calm the butterflies. Upstairs, on the second floor, the bride and her bridesmaids were busy getting ready for the ceremony. The bride was a beautiful young woman, with long brown hair and a wedding dress that had a train over ten feet long. She had never felt so happy, and she and her bridal party talked and laughed together, filled with excitement.

Remember that this is 1834, so a great deal of the lighting was still provided by candles. Amid all the happy goings-on, no one noticed a candle fall over. No one noticed that candle start a small fire, a fire that quickly spread over the old wooden floors and the window curtains. Suddenly, the bride let out a bloodcurdling scream, for the flames had reached her wedding dress train. The bridesmaids quickly surrounded the bride, trying to put out the fire on her dress, noticing too late that the room was rapidly becoming engulfed by fire until there was no escape.

Meanwhile, downstairs, the groom didn't notice anything was wrong—until he began to smell the smoke coming from the fire on the second floor. And then he began to hear the screams, the screams of his bride-to-be and her bridesmaids trapped upstairs in the fire, burning to death. The groom ran like lightning to the staircase that would lead him up the second floor, determined to rescue them. But then he saw that the staircase was itself already consumed by fire, and there was no hope of rescue. His friends had to drag him out of the City Tavern by force to save his life, and the groom could do nothing but stand outside, watching the building burn and listening as, one by one, the screams stopped. The bride and all her bridesmaids were killed in the fire at the City Tavern on that tragic day in March 1834. From that point on, the once lively and vital building stood empty and silent, and its sad ruins were demolished twenty years later, in 1854.

But, as I said, when they rebuilt and re-created the City Tavern, they resurrected its spirits. And ever since the building opened again to the public in 1976, staff and diners have seen the ghostly apparition of a beautiful woman with brown hair, wearing a wedding dress from another time. Sometimes people have seen her on the tavern's staircase—the staircase leading from the first floor to the second—one hand reaching out as if pleading for help before disappearing. One patron in the 1990s went into the bathroom on the second floor alone, and when she looked in the mirror, there was a strange woman standing right behind her. When she turned around, there was no one there. On the second floor, glasses of water often fall over by themselves, untouched by human hands, and candles are mysteriously extinguished, as if the ghost of the bride is trying to prevent another tragedy like the one that cruelly took her life nearly two hundred years ago.

Weddings were often held at the City Tavern after it was reopened in 1976, and there has been a startling amount of wedding photographs of bridal parties taken on the second floor that have one unusual thing in common. When people look at the photograph afterward, they notice a woman standing in the back of the group. She is a beautiful young woman with long brown hair, and she is smiling, just like the rest. But no one recognizes this woman. No one remembers her being there when the picture was taken. But in the photograph, she is there.

Many believe this is the ghost of the Bride of City Tavern, hoping, in vain, that this happy day was hers, trying to capture some of the joy that was tragically denied her during her lifetime.

THE REBORN CITY TAVERN, after forty-four years, sadly closed "permanently" in 2020 due to the ongoing COVID-19 pandemic. In an article for the *Philadelphia Inquirer*, Chef Walter Staib, who ran the restaurant for the past twenty-six years and brought the City Tavern to national attention with his thirteen-Emmy-award-winning PBS television series *A Taste of History*, said of the closure: "In one sentence, this is bittersweet." The City Tavern's last day of operation was, fittingly, October 31, 2020—Halloween. I happened to be doing the Ghost Tour of Philadelphia that night and saw the City Tavern ablaze with lights and heard the laughter from the multitudes inside echoing as I told my stories of its haunted past. On November 2, 2020, it was announced to the public the City Tavern had closed forever. It was a huge shock. That a place that had become such a successful Philly institution could suddenly vanish overnight—I wonder if that's how people felt back in 1834.

When I tell the ghost stories of the City Tavern now, as of this writing, the building remains dark and deserted. But given its incredible history, I have faith that the tavern will rise from the ashes again one day, as it has more than once in its illustrious past.

Until that day comes, the spirits of the City Tavern have it all to themselves. Visit it if you can, and make sure you look in the windows at night. You never know what you might see.

CHAPTER 3

PHANTOMS PROTECTING THE POWEL HOUSE

Many fine old houses still exist in the neighborhood known as Society Hill, but there is one located at 244 South Third Street that is special—it is the only building on the block that predates the American Revolution. It is now known as the Powel House, and visiting the home today for a historic tour allows visitors to step back into eighteenth-century Philadelphia, walking on the same wooden floorboards traversed by the most influential men and women of the era, including George and Martha Washington, John and Abigail Adams, Ben Franklin, the Marquis de Lafayette and, of course, Samuel and Elizabeth Powel themselves. Built in 1765 by Charles Stedman (who never lived in it) and meticulously restored after being saved from a wrecking ball in the twentieth century, the Powel House is one of the city's most significant house museums, operated by the Philadelphia Society for the Preservation of Landmarks. With such incredible history witnessed within its walls, it is no surprise that some of that extraordinary energy from the past should remain behind, causing the Powel House to also be known as one of Philadelphia's most haunted houses.

Samuel Powel belonged to one of the city's most prominent families, his grandfather having immigrated to Philadelphia in 1685. Born in 1738, he inherited the bulk of the family's money and land when he turned eighteen years old. Like many young men and women of means in the eighteenth century, Samuel Powel embarked on the Grand Tour of Europe. Powel was so enthralled by what he found there that he stayed abroad not for the usual one or two years but for seven, meeting many famous figures, including the

Exterior of the Powel House. *Photo by Beyond My Ken. Wikimedia Commons.*

writer Voltaire and the pope. When he finally returned to Philadelphia, he soon married Elizabeth Willing, the daughter of another one of the city's elite families. Their wedding took place on August 7, 1769, at Christ Church. Instead of moving into one of the ninety different pieces of property he then owned, Samuel Powel purchased the elegant house on Third Street, after which he and his wife, Elizabeth, transformed it into one of the great showplaces of the era. Samuel held the office of mayor of Philadelphia twice; he served his first term from 1775 to 1776, as Philadelphia's last mayor before the revolution, and his second from 1789 to 1790, after which he became of a member of the United States Senate.

Born on February 21, 1743, Elizabeth Willing Powel, known as Eliza, was one of the most extraordinarily influential women of her time. Although women were, of course, not able to hold elected office, Eliza is the one who made the Powel House the center of philosophical, political and social life in colonial Philadelphia. Ferociously intelligent and well-read, Eliza could hold her own with anyone in conversation and was never afraid to offer her own opinions about current events. Virtually everyone who ever met her was awed by her. Even Eliza's sister, Ann, wrote in a letter about her "uncommon command" of language and ideas. A French marquis who served in the American Revolution named François-Jean de Chastellux wrote in his memoirs that "contrary to American custom, she plays the leading role in the family…but what chiefly distinguishes her is her taste for conversation…in which she uses her wit and knowledge." Of the marriage between Eliza and Samuel Powel, Chastellux said they lived together in "perfect equality…unusually well-matched in understanding, taste, and knowledge."

When Abigail Adams arrived in Philadelphia, she met Eliza Powel and said in a letter that "of all the ladies I have seen and conversed with here, Mrs. Powel is the best informed. She is a friendly, affable, good woman, sprightly, full of conversation, a woman of many charms." John Adams wrote a letter on September 8, 1774, describing the luxury of a meal at the Powel House, which was never anything less than a major event, with guests including the most influential figures of the time. His letter reads: "Dined at Mr. Powel's….A most sinful feast again! Every thing which could delight the eye, or allure the taste, curds and creams, jellies, sweet meats of various sorts, twenty sorts of tarts, fools, trifles, floating islands…Parmesan cheese, punch, wine, porter, beer, etc. etc." After this "sinful feast" and much drinking, John Adams and several other guests decided to get a view of the city by climbing the steeple of Christ Church, which was at that time the tallest man-made structure in the colonies.

Eliza Powel was also an extremely close friend of George and Martha Washington, who were both frequent visitors to the home and even celebrated their twentieth wedding anniversary in the ballroom of the Powel House. Many scholars believe that it was Eliza's letter to George Washington that convinced him to run for a second term as president of the United States. He had revealed to her that he planned to retire after his first term, leaving Eliza's mind "thrown into a train of reflections in consequence of the sentiments that you had confided to me." Eliza wrote him a passionate letter arguing it was necessary for him to continue. It reads, in part:

> *Will you withdraw your Aid from a Structure that certainly wants your Assistance to support it? Can you, with Fortitude, see it crumble to decay? I know you cannot you will not....I will venture to assert that, at this Time, you are the only Man in America that dares to do right on all public Occasions. You are called to watch over the Welfare of a great People at a Period of Life when Man is capable of sustaining the Weight of Government. You have shewn that you are not to be intoxicated by Power or misled by Flattery. You have a feeling Heart, and the long Necessity of behaving with Circumspection must have tempered that native Benevolence which otherwise might make you too compliant, the Soundness of your Judgement has been evinced on many and trying Occasions, and you have frequently demonstrated that you possess an Empire over yourself. For Gods sake do not yield that Empire to a Love of Ease, Retirement, rural Pursuits, or a false Diffidence of Abilities which those that best know you so justly appreciate; nay your very Figure is calculated to inspire Respect and Confidence in the People, whose simple good Sense associates the noblest qualities of Mind with the heroic Form when it is embellished by such remarkable Tenets of Mildness and calm Benevolence—and such I believe was the first Intention of Nature.*

George Washington never answered this letter, but it is clear that he listened and followed her advice. He was elected to a second term, and their friendship continued unabated. Washington viewed Eliza as an equal in a way that was refreshing for the time, always ending his letters to her "with the greatest respect and affection"; Eliza, in turn, ended hers with "Your sincere affectionate friend." Ten days after George Washington's death in 1799, Eliza, herself a widow by this time, was one of the first people to write to Martha Washington with her condolences, concluding her letter with the words, "I have lost a much-valued friend."

Despite her immense influence and power in society, Eliza Powel's life was also marked by personal tragedies that threw her into deep depressions. She had four children with Samuel Powel between 1771 and 1775, all of whom were stillborn or died within a few weeks of disease. Eliza kept locks of two of her children's hair and wrote frankly of her extreme sorrow in letters, mourning the loss of "my beloved angels." In 1783, she wrote:

Ah my dear Friend there are no Roses without Thorns. You wish me to be again a Mother, you know not what you wish. Indeed I am no longer what you once knew me. Those fine Spirits, that I used to flatter myself would never be broken, have at length yielded to the too severe Trials that have assailed me. My Mind, habituated to Mortification & Disappointment, is become weaker, &, unfortunately, my Sensibilities stronger. A thousand Circumstances that formerly were Sources of Pleasure to me have now lost their Charm. Time does not lessen real Griefs. In some Instances it augments them by removing to a greater distance the Objects on which our Happiness depends. I fear I am doomed never to be happy in this World.

Ten years later, on September 29, 1793, Samuel Powel died in the yellow fever epidemic. Eliza Powel never married again and sold the Powel House to William Bingham in 1798, moving into a mansion on Chestnut Street for the final decades of her life. Although she had no living biological children, Eliza was extremely fond of her nephew John Powel Hare, whom she had cared for when he came down with scarlet fever as an infant. She made him her heir, and he later changed his name to John Hare Powel. A month before her death, guests at a dinner party noted Eliza's emotional distress as she confronted her mortality, saying, "Have I ever done good in my life? Can people go to Heaven without doing good?"

Eliza Willing Powel died on January 17, 1830, at the age of eighty-six. As part of her last will and testament, she left an annual bequest of one hundred dollars to the Pennsylvania Abolition Society that was to continue for twenty years, along with a message: "I feel it to be the duty of every individual to cooperate by all honorable means in the abolition of slavery, and in the restoration of freedom to that important part of the family of mankind, which has so long groaned under oppression." Eliza Powel is buried next to her husband, Samuel, in Christ Church Burial Ground. Her epitaph reads: "Distinguished by her good sense and her good works."

By the early years of the twentieth century, the Powel House had entered into a state of decay, serving as a warehouse for a business that imported horsehair. In 1918, the original woodwork and plaster of the withdrawing room was sold to the Metropolitan Museum of Art, and in 1925, the same elements of the ballroom were given to the Philadelphia Museum of Art. Five years later, in 1930, the Powel House was slated to be demolished and turned into a parking lot for taxicabs. A prominent Philadelphian named

Frances Anne Wister was determined to save it, despite the house's poor condition, and she enlisted others to her cause. She wrote:

> *The plight of the mansion, far from deterring us, aroused a determination to save it....Rooms of noble proportions, and the last house in the "Old City" where Washington was a frequent guest. It would have been a crime to destroy this historic mansion where the feet of so many patriots trod; a place which was the center for all the important people of the time in national and local history.*

The efforts of Frances Ann Wister, a woman as extraordinary as Eliza Powel in many ways, were successful and led to the creation of the Philadelphia Society for the Preservation of Landmarks. Frances Wister wrote, "Long were our deliberations over the selection of a president. I naturally assumed that some prominent man would be found who would undertake this job, and nobody was more surprised than myself when the Committee invited me to be that prominent man." The Powel House interiors were restored to their original eighteenth-century glory, and it opened to the public as a museum in 1938, with a site manager always living on the property.

The lore about the Powel House being haunted originates from an article written by Barbara Barnes for the *Philadelphia Bulletin* entitled "Philadelphia's Haunted Houses—Old and New," which was fittingly published on October 31, 1965. In this article, site managers Edwin Coutant Moore and his wife, Anne Djorup Moore, described the ghostly encounters they both experienced while living in the Powel House, which they did for sixteen years, from 1951 until Edwin Moore died in 1967, just two years after this article was published. I quote from this article below; the following text appeared under the heading "The Powel House Mystery." Note that when Edwin and Anne Moore describe the drawing room in the article, they are referring to what is now called the ballroom on the second floor of the house. A photograph accompanying the original article, showing Anne Moore where she witnessed a spirit, proves this.

> *"One day I was descending the front staircase," reports Edwin Coutant Moore, historian who lives at the Powel House, 244 S. 3rd Street. "I glanced ahead and two young officers were coming up toward me. I can still see them distinctly," Moore insists. "One wore a blue uniform. He looked up and smiled pleasantly. His teeth were very white. Suddenly he was*

Entrance hall of the Powel House. *Photo by the Historic American Buildings Survey. Public domain.*

gone." It was Mrs. Moore who saw "my pretty lady," as she now calls her, at dusk in the drawing room. "She was fanning and tapping her foot," the historian's wife recalls. "Her black hair was piled high with pearls. Her dress was beige and lavender. She looked directly at me. When I snapped on the light, the chair where she had been was empty." But months later, when Mrs. Moore tried to rent a Colonial costume for a party, she was shown a "Peggy Shippen gown." "It was the very same beige and lavender dress. I almost fainted," she says.

The Moores are not in the least disturbed by the spirits with whom they apparently share their home. "This is a happy place," they say.

"It always has been. In the old days everyone of consequence came here. George Washington, Thomas Jefferson, Benjamin Franklin were frequent visitors." So was the Marquis de Lafayette. And Moore feels it may have been he who was ascending the staircase. Only rarely does the dog bark when noises are heard. Mostly the noises are normal creakings of an old house. "But sometimes if you turn the light on suddenly in the big drawing room, the whole floor squeaks as if a lot of people were hurriedly leaving," says Moore. The antique wardrobe in the Moores' bedroom has a habit of opening about four in the morning. And if it is locked, the door creaks loudly about the same time. Moore once lived in "an unfriendly house" in New York. "You were afraid to walk around in it. Sometimes you felt as if something were rushing past you," he says. His 14 years at the Powel House he terms, "very happy and friendly." Asked if he believes in ghosts he says, "No. But I don't disbelieve either."

While many have taken Anne Moore's story to mean that Peggy Shippen, known in history as the wife of Benedict Arnold, is the "pretty lady" haunting the house, it seems unlikely. Others speculate that the ghostly presence seen and felt in the ballroom and the drawing room is Eliza Powel herself, as many site managers and psychics have detected her presence there. Although she did not die inside the house, it would make sense that she might sometimes return to the home she lived in with her husband for so many years and where she experienced the devastating loss of her children. The sound of footsteps on the front staircase has been experienced by many visitors and staff members over the years. When I went to the Powel House for a tour in January 2022, I spoke with docent Judy Smith, education and programs coordinator Mackenzie Warren and executive director Kayla Anthony about their personal experiences in the house. As we were talking about the peculiar sound of footsteps, Judy Smith turned to me and said, "It happened today just before you came."

Former executive director Jonathan Burton began his time working with PhilaLandmarks as the site manager for the Powel House. Over the years, I had many conversations with him about lights being found turned on when he had definitely turned them off and alarms being triggered in the house, only for him to find no one there and nothing out of place. Mickey Herr and her husband, Chip, also spent many years as site managers living in the Powel House, and Mickey and I shared a long conversation about the haunting and who she thinks the resident ghost might be:

I have a theory about who the main ghost is in the house. After leaving, I continued to be connected to the house, especially in researching Powel House through time. I have given a lot of thought to who else lived there through its more than 250-year existence. And the story of Edwin Moore really struck me. My earliest experience with the house, when I moved in and I was home alone, I always got the sense that I was never alone. When I would perform my museum duties, like checking humidity readings or opening blinds, in the beginning, I was a bit nervous. Am I doing it correctly? And it felt like someone was following me. Watching what I was doing to make sure I did it right. It didn't dawn on me until much later. Of course, Edwin! He really wanted to create the colonial ambiance, and he wanted to keep everything the same.

I can say that when we lived there, Chip had an experience where he was walking from the apartment at the back through the museum to the front door; he was leaving early for work, and it was at the time of year when the hallway is still very dark. As he was fumbling with the original locks, he heard somebody walking down the stairs behind him. And you think about Edwin's stories of Lafayette and the soldiers. But what if it was actually Edwin Moore coming downstairs: "Who's at my door?" It makes sense that he would always be vetting the new site managers. Chip had a few things that felt as if someone was looking after him. He was in the ballroom on a tall ladder underneath the chandelier, changing lightbulbs, and he said somebody grabbed his ankle. He looked down, and no one was in the room. When we talked about it later, it made sense that someone had been trying to help: "OK, you're doing something good; let's make sure you do it right." When we first moved in, a lot of weird things happened. The door on the third floor going up into the attic was alarmed, and it was really hard to open. It would get stuck. And when we were in our apartment, that door would just open and set the alarms off. But then it stopped. It's easy to believe all these other spirits could be in the house, but who else but Edwin Coutant Moore would want to see how you react when the alarms go off?

In addition to his many years living at the Powel House, Edwin Coutant Moore was also the founder of the Colonial Philadelphia Historical Society. He died on October 31, 1967, two years to the day since the article was published in the *Philadelphia Bulletin*. After being the first person to publicize the haunting of the Powel House, did Edwin Moore return after his death to watch over the house? I must confess, it seems extremely

Front parlor of the Powel House. *Photo by the Historic American Buildings Survey. Public domain.*

likely to me. The ghosts of the Powel House have never felt malevolent to anyone; it is more a feeling of protection, which would make sense if it is indeed Moore who is the primary spirit. Kayla Anthony told me that several people over the years have seen the apparition of a man wearing a top hat in the house, appearing in silhouette. I shared with her that I had also seen this same figure. A few years ago, I was leading a ghost tour inside the Powel House, and I was standing on the second-floor landing, telling guests about the ballroom, which we were about to enter. I noticed the silhouette of a man standing on the stairs leading up to the third floor, which is roped off and not open to the public. I didn't feel afraid in the moment; it just felt like someone was watching to see what I was doing, and then the figure disappeared. Could this have been Edwin Moore's ghost? It makes sense to me that it might have been.

There is one more spirit that has been encountered inside the Powel House that is not human; it is the ghost of a cat. One former site manager chased a cat through the house until it simply vanished, and people on ghost tours, including myself, have also seen it. Mickey Herr had an answer for this haunting as well, because it was her cat, Maggie Mae, who lived with her and her husband, Chip, while they were site managers at the Powel House:

My cat, Maggie Mae, had been with me even before I married Chip. She was a Hoboken street cat I adopted. When we moved to the Powel House, she had the ultimate city garden, right? And she had always been a scaredy-cat; if the doorbell rang, she would hide under the bed. But when we moved into the Powel House, Maggie changed. She became a different cat. She was very proud of the Powel House, and she was very proud of the garden. When tourists would come to the gate, not only would she not hide, she would "prounce" over to the gate as if to say, "This is my garden." She was out there as much as she could be; she owned that garden. When we were getting ready to move [out], Maggie was quite old and on her last legs, and I knew it was time to say goodbye. I wanted to surreptitiously bury her in that garden, but she ended up dying two days later and several blocks away in our new apartment on Pine Street. It was two years later when a new site manager told me the story [of chasing a cat through the house]. I asked him to describe the cat; I was shocked when he said, "Skinny, black and white," which sounded to me like Maggie Mae. And I thought, "Well, apparently just because she didn't die there didn't mean she didn't go right back." She was a lovely cat. She was the spirit. She loved that place so much.

The Powel House is an essential place to visit for anyone who is interested in the history of Philadelphia, and the Philadelphia Society for the Preservation of Landmarks is extremely worthy of your support. Go take a tour someday and step back in time to the eighteenth century, and if you're lucky, you may come face-to-face with one of its ghostly past residents who loved the house dearly and is still watching over it after death. What Edwin and Anne Moore said in 1965 still rings true today: "This is a happy place; it always has been." When you visit the Powel House, you might also want to bring a little treat for Maggie Mae, just in case.

CHAPTER 4

NIGHT TERRORS
AT INDEPENDENCE HALL

The Pennsylvania State House, which we now know better as Independence Hall, is without question the most significant historic site in the city of Philadelphia and arguably the most significant in the United States of America. For within this building, the Second Continental Congress met. Here the Declaration of Independence was debated and signed in 1776, and here the Constitution was debated and signed in 1787. So, within the walls of this elegant building on Chestnut Street between Fifth and Sixth Streets, the United States of America was born. With such momentous historical events taking place here, it is no surprise that Independence Hall is haunted by ghostly echoes from the distant past.

Construction of the State House took twenty-one years, from 1732 to 1753, since it was built as funds were made available. Designed by Andrew Hamilton (the original "Philadelphia lawyer") and Edmund Wooley, who actually constructed the building, the structure we now call Independence Hall is a masterpiece of Georgian architecture. The central structure of the State House contains the Assembly Room and the home of the original Supreme Court, topped by a tower that climbs 168 feet into the sky. There are two other wings connected to the State House. On the Sixth Street side of the building is Congress Hall, home of the House of Representatives and the Senate from 1790 to 1800, and on the Fifth Street side is Old City Hall, home of the original Supreme Court for the same period. Taken all together, these three buildings housed the entirety of the United States government as the nation was in its infancy. The President's House was one block north on Market Street.

Independence Hall at night.

Independence Hall is, of course, a primary stop on the Ghost Tour of Philadelphia, and I have told its stories many hundreds of times over the past fifteen years. Every once in a while, I take a moment to simply stand there, looking at the building, and remind myself of where I am. Living and working in Philadelphia, it is easy to walk past these hallowed landmarks and not give them a second thought, but I think it's important to remember just how momentous it is to visit this building in particular, the true birthplace of the idea of what this country could be. Many years, I have done the ghost tour on July 4, and I always find myself moved as I speak about this place. Moved, and sometimes deeply unnerved. It's in moments like these that you can feel the past almost as a physical presence, the many ghosts of Philadelphia's history watching your every move, listening to your every word, making sure you tell their stories true and well.

> Resolved: That these United Colonies are, and of right ought to be, free and independent States, that they are absolved from all allegiance to the British Crown, and that all political connection between them and the State of Great Britain is, and ought to be, totally dissolved.
>
> That it is expedient forthwith to take the most effectual measures for forming foreign Alliances.
>
> That a plan of confederation be prepared and transmitted to the respective Colonies for their consideration and approbation.

These words, written by Richard Henry Lee on June 7, 1776, are known as the Lee Resolution, the first active political step towards the thirteen North American colonies separating themselves from England as an independent nation. Several weeks earlier, a similar but more radical resolution had been presented to Congress by John Adams of Massachusetts on May 15, 1776. Congress had passed Adams's motion, but four of the colonies voted against it, and the delegates from Maryland walked out of Congress in protest. Although Adams himself wrote of his resolution of May 15, "This day the Congress has passed the most important resolution that was ever taken in America," the fact that there was already much dissension between the delegates of Congress was not fortuitous for the cause of independence.

Therefore, it fell to Richard Henry Lee, the highly respected delegate from the colony of Virginia, to try again, and this time the words were heard and accepted. Although he was as passionate about the cause of American independence as John Adams was, Lee was a cultured gentleman of Virginia whose opinions carried much weight throughout the colonies, especially in the south. Adams was a fiery, opinionated patriot not ashamed to make his voice heard, but he was also a shrewd politician. When Richard Henry Lee made his motion arguing independence to Congress, John Adams seconded the motion.

Lee's resolution led to the creation of the Committee of Five just a few days later, on June 11, 1776, to oversee the writing of what would soon become known as the Declaration of Independence. This committee included two future presidents of the United States, John Adams of Massachusetts and Thomas Jefferson of Virginia; Benjamin Franklin of Pennsylvania, one of the most revered intellectuals, politicians and citizens of his age; as well as two other men who are not as famous but are just as significant: Roger Sherman of Connecticut—who is the only person to sign all four of the documents leading to the creation of the United States as we know it (the Continental Association, the Declaration of Independence, the Articles of Confederation and the Constitution)—and Robert Livingston of New York, who later served as the first secretary of foreign affairs, administered the very first presidential oath of office for George Washington in 1789 and later still negotiated the Louisiana Purchase with France.

All five were great men of their time and moment, with wildly different backgrounds and temperaments, but they were all drawn together in this fraught moment with a common mission: to create a document that would make the idea of an independent United States of America an undeniable and necessary reality to Congress, the citizens of the colonies and the world at large—especially King George III in England. It was quickly decided that the writing of this document be primarily delegated to Thomas Jefferson, another Virginian whose voice would undoubtedly be heard. Jefferson was initially reluctant to undertake the task of writing the Declaration of Independence, understandably so. But John Adams, ever practical, did something very sensible to get Jefferson to agree he was the best man for the job—he took him to the City Tavern and got him drunk. After a few rounds of liquid courage, Thomas Jefferson said yes.

He didn't have much time. Jefferson wrote the initial draft of the Declaration of Independence in just seventeen days. To have the privacy and quiet he needed, he temporarily moved into the second floor of a small house owned by Jacob Graff at Seventh and High (now Market) Streets, which was at the time considered the outskirts of Philadelphia, even though it was only one block away from the Pennsylvania State House. Thomas Jefferson rented the second floor of this house, which consisted of a parlor and a bedroom, for thirty-five shillings a week.

Accompanying Thomas Jefferson to Philadelphia that eventful summer of 1776 was an enslaved boy only fourteen years old by the name of Robert "Bob" Hemings. Robert's sister, Sally Hemings, was also an enslaved African owned by Jefferson, sexually assaulted by him, who bore Jefferson many children whose descendants still live today. George W. Boudreau writes of Robert "Bob" Hemings in his book *Independence: A Guide to Historic Philadelphia*:

> *We have no record of fourteen-year-old Bob Hemings' reaction to Philadelphia, no clues if he wondered why his owner's famous statement that "all men are created equal" did not apply to him. What we do know of Bob was that his labor was a valuable asset to Jefferson that summer, as he took care of laundry and ran countless errands. We can tell from Jefferson's meticulous account books that he rewarded his slave's special duties with the purchase of items of clothing, including shoes and stockings, which were not provided to field hands. Bob Hemings also probably had the opportunity to meet members of Philadelphia's large free and enslaved African American community, an experience that was far different than that of living in slave quarters or plantations…. The work Bob Hemings did that summer, while living in the Graff house, allowed his owner to maintain a comfortable life and enjoy the city. Like many of the men who proclaimed freedom that summer, Thomas Jefferson was cared for by an enslaved American.*

The Assembly Room at Independence Hall. *Photo by xiquinhosilva. Wikimedia Commons.*

It is also important to note, because it almost never is mentioned in history books, that while the delegates of the Second Continental Congress were debating the issue of independence in the Assembly Room of the Pennsylvania State House, in the hallway outside of that hallowed chamber there stood and sat many enslaved Africans, ready to respond to any wishes their white "masters" commanded while they were engaged in their most important congressional business. Robert "Bob" Hemings, bound in slavery to Thomas Jefferson, was almost certainly one of them. James Madison recalled in 1787,

> *Whilst the last members were signing it* [the Constitution] *Doctor FRANKLIN, looking towards the Presidents Chair, at the back of which a rising sun happened to be painted, observed to a few members near him, that Painters had found it difficult to distinguish in their art a rising from a setting sun. "I have," said he, "often and often in the course of the Session, and the vicissitudes of my hopes and fears as to its issue, looked at that painted sun behind the President without being able to tell whether it was rising or setting: But now at length I have the happiness to know that it is a rising and not a setting Sun."*

It was James Madison, another Virginian, who made the most significant contributions to the Constitutional Convention of 1787. Madison was dissatisfied with what he regarded as the weak national government established by the earlier Articles of Confederation, and his proposal, known as the Virginia Plan, was used as the template for the creation of the three branches of United States government called for in the eventual United States Constitution.

Despite the heat and humidity of a typical Philadelphia summer, Congress kept the windows of the State House Assembly Room closed so no passersby could hear their debate. As the time for signing the new Constitution drew near, Ben Franklin was approached in the street by Elizabeth Willing Powel. She asked him, "Well, Doctor, what have we got? A republic or a monarchy?" Franklin replied to her with an answer and a warning: "A republic…if you can keep it."

Philadelphia ceased to be the center of United States government in 1800, and afterward the State House lost its immediate political significance. It did not stand empty, however. Charles Willson Peale turned the Long Gallery on the second floor into the nation's first museum, filled with his paintings of notable figures of the time and relics of natural history, including the full skeleton of a mastodon. In 1822, Peale painted a self-portrait called *The Artist in His Museum*, featuring him raising a red curtain to reveal the portraits and exhibitions displayed in the Long Gallery of Independence Hall. Now on display at the Pennsylvania Academy of the Fine Arts, this painting gives us a glimpse of what the building looked like during this time.

In 1824, the Marquis de Lafayette returned to visit Philadelphia for the first time in many years, saying, "My entrance through this fair and great city amidst the most solemn and affecting recollections…has excited emotions in my heart in which are mingled the feeling of nearly fifty years." It was during the preparation for the Marquis de Lafayette's visit to the State House that those organizing his reception began to refer to it as "the hall of Independence." It is from this time that the Pennsylvania State House gained the nickname for which it is now best known.

On his inaugural journey to Washington, President-elect Abraham Lincoln stopped in Philadelphia and visited Independence Hall on February 22, 1861. He was not expecting to make a speech, but he did, and his words have a particular poignancy and prophecy in hindsight:

> *I am filled with deep emotion at finding myself standing here, in this place, where were collected together the wisdom, the patriotism, the devotion to principle, from which sprang the institutions under which we live. You have kindly suggested to me that in my hands is the task of restoring peace to the*

present distracted condition of the country. I can say in return, Sir, that all the political sentiments I entertain have been drawn, so far as I have been able to draw them, from the sentiments which originated and were given to the world from this hall. I have never had a feeling politically that did not spring from the sentiments embodied in the Declaration of Independence. I have often pondered over the dangers which were incurred by the men who assembled here and framed and adopted that Declaration of Independence. I have pondered over the toils that were endured by the officers and soldiers of the army who achieved that Independence. I have often inquired of myself, what great principle or idea it was that kept this Confederacy so long together. It was not the mere matter of the separation of the Colonies from the motherland; but that sentiment in the Declaration of Independence which gave liberty, not alone to the people of this country, but, I hope, to the world, for all future time. It was that which gave promise that in due time the weight would be lifted from the shoulders of all men. This is a sentiment embodied in the Declaration of Independence. Now, my friends, can this country be saved upon that basis? If it can, I will consider myself one of the happiest men in the world, if I can help to save it. If it cannot be saved upon that principle, it will be truly awful. But if this country cannot be saved without giving up that principle, I was about to say I would rather be assassinated on this spot than surrender it.

A little over four years later, on April 22, 1865, the corpse of the assassinated president Abraham Lincoln arrived in Philadelphia and lay in state in the Assembly Room of Independence Hall. Over three hundred thousand mourners came to view his body, many of them waiting in line for hours to pay their final respects to the man who concluded his impromptu speech in front of the hall four years earlier with the words: "I have said nothing but what I am willing to live by and, if it be the pleasure of Almighty God, die by." The ghost of Abraham Lincoln is the one seen and felt most often at the White House, and his phantom funeral train is said to still trace its mournful route from Washington to Illinois on the anniversary of his death.

In 1948, Independence Hall was restored to its eighteenth-century appearance, and Congress ordered the creation of Independence National Historical Park the same year. Throughout the twentieth century, Independence Hall continued to be a symbolic meeting place for peaceful protest used by the women of the suffrage movement and by men and women of the Civil Rights Movement. The LGBTQ rights movement also began here at Independence Hall. The first "Annual Reminder" was held in front of the building on July 4, 1965, with men and women dressed in business attire to show the world that homosexuals were just like everyone else silently picketing and holding signs demanding their rights as promised in the Declaration of Independence: "Life, liberty, and the pursuit of happiness."

The final Annual Reminder rally took place on July 4, 1969, only a few days after the Stonewall uprising in New York City became the launching pad for the modern LGBTQ rights movement, showing that the time for silent protest was over. In 2005, a Pennsylvania State Historical Marker was placed in front of Independence Hall to commemorate the brave people who first began to march for their rights in Philadelphia, four years before Stonewall.

Independence Hall is home to many spirits from the past, many of which have been seen and experienced by the park rangers and security guards who keep the building safe from harm.

In 1943, a security guard related to a local newspaper that he had been on duty at night, alone in Independence Hall—or so he believed. While on his regular patrol, he saw the door to the Assembly Room open by itself, and then the misty figure of a man began to appear in the doorway. The security guard left the building. Other people from the mid-twentieth century reported seeing the ghost of Benjamin Franklin himself pacing up and down the hallways in the dead of the night, deep in thought.

The Long Gallery on the second floor is another haunted hot spot at Independence Hall. A park ranger I interviewed for this book on the condition of anonymity told the story that one day they were in the Long Gallery when they heard a man coughing and then saying the words "Help me" in a voice that was gasping for breath. No one was there. There is ample reason why this area of the building should be haunted—during the British occupation of Philadelphia in 1777, the second floor was used as a hospital for prisoners of war, and the conditions were horrific. Colonel Persifor Frazer later wrote of his confinement at the Pennsylvania State House:

Many of us were here for six days without having any provision served to us—and for many weeks after, our allowance did not exceed from 4 to 6 ounces of salt pork and about half a pound of very ordinary biscuit per day—and had it not been for the supply we had from the citizens we must have all inevitably perished....There were forty of us in the two upper chambers of the State House.

When restoration work was done on the Long Gallery, crews found wooden beams below the floorboards that were stained with the blood of prisoners from the time of the American Revolution. Once Congress returned to Independence Hall in 1778, Congressional President Henry Laurens remarked on

the offensiveness of the air around the State House, which the enemy had made a hospital and left in a condition disgraceful....Particularly they had opened a large pit near the House, a receptacle for filth, into which they also cast dead horses and the bodies of men who by the mercy of death had escaped from their further cruelties.

The exact location of this mass grave near Independence Hall is not recorded, but it makes sense that the ghosts of some who perished inside of the building may never have left it.

Another park ranger I was able to interview said they had often heard footsteps walking through the building at night when no one was found, and occasionally experienced the smell of tobacco or cigar smoke. The park ranger took all this in stride, but there was one night when the ghosts of Independence Hall were especially active:

I was in the hall by myself, and it had been a pretty routine night, which is to say it was pretty boring. I was walking around on the first floor when, all of a sudden, I heard guys talking in the Assembly Room. Like, I heard a lot of guys talking, shouting over each other, laughing. I couldn't make out what any of the words were because there were so many talking at the same time. And I just froze for a minute, because like...this couldn't be happening. There's no one here but me. Then I got myself together and walked over to the door, and then it got quiet. I'm not sure, but I think I heard someone say "Shhhh!" like they knew someone was coming. Then I started to get freaked out because I know there's something behind that door, even though there couldn't be, you know? So, I opened the door and there was not a single person in that room. No one. And I think I'm losing it. I closed the door and took a few steps, and then the voices started talking again. I just looked at the door, and I was like, "No way I'm opening it again." I walked outside and stood there until my relief came. And this was in January, it was

The stairwell of Independence Hall. *Photo by xiquinhosilva. Wikimedia Commons.*

freezing cold outside, but no way was I going back in there alone. About an hour later, a buddy of mine came, and I told them what happened, expecting them to think I've lost it and report me or whatever. But they just kind of laughed and were like, "Oh yeah, that happens." And I was like, "Oh, OK then." It only happened to me that one time, though.

Perhaps the most terrifying supernatural encounter to happen inside of Independence Hall was experienced by two park rangers in 2002. According to Tim Reeser's book *Ghost Stories of Philadelphia, PA*, the two men were standing outside the front door of the building just after sunset. It was dark, and all the tourists were long gone. Independence Hall was locked up tight, empty. But perhaps not so empty after all. The two park rangers both heard a message on their radios from headquarters, saying, "There's a breach of security inside Independence Hall. The motion sensors are picking up somebody walking around."

Immediately, the two men sprang into action. They went inside and searched Independence Hall from top to bottom. But there was no intruder to be found. Nothing was out of place; everything was just as it should have been. Thinking that maybe they were being subjected to a practical joke or a surprise training exercise, after concluding their search, they radioed back to headquarters: "All clear at Independence Hall. No one's here except for us."

Almost as soon as those words left the park rangers' lips, they received another radio call from headquarters, this time even more emphatic: "No, there's someone walking around on the second floor. It's a man, we saw him on the security cameras just for a second but then we lost him. He hasn't been seen leaving through any of the doors, so he's got to be hiding in the building somewhere. You two guys have got to find him!"

So, the two park rangers searched Independence Hall a second time, searching any place a man could conceivably be hiding, checking underneath every table, behind every door…and still they found nobody there. Frustrated now, they radioed back to headquarters and said: "Look, we just can't find this man you're talking about. We've looked everywhere and there's no one. Check the security cameras again. If you see the intruder, just tell us where he is, and we'll grab him!"

Then there was a very long silence, and the two park rangers stood there, waiting alone in the dark. And then headquarters radioed back to them, and it turned out to be the last time headquarters had contact with those two park rangers that night. Headquarters said: "We're looking at you two guys on the security cameras right now, and the intruder is standing right beside you!"

The two men looked around them—and there was nobody there. But then they heard something: footsteps coming down the staircase behind them. They quickly turned around, ready to catch the intruder they had been searching for, but the staircase was empty. Yet they still heard the sound of footsteps, coming closer and closer toward them. And then a man began to materialize on the staircase, a man wearing clothing that looked like they were from the colonial days. The man on the stairs was staggering, slowly walking down the stairs toward the park rangers.

The park rangers looked at one another to make sure they were both seeing the same thing on the stairs, and then they ran out of Independence Hall, into the night. They called the next day and said they were resigning, effective immediately. Neither one of them has set foot anywhere near Independence Hall again since that night of terror.

Many suspect that the specter witnessed by the two park rangers that night was the ghost of a man by the name of Joseph Fry. He was a doorkeeper at the Pennsylvania State House who lived in a small room in the western wing. On August 29, 1793, Joseph Fry was found dead in his room, a victim of the yellow fever epidemic, his body covered in the blood and black vomit characteristic of the disease. This was a month into the yellow fever epidemic of 1793, and before this, most of the deaths had occurred in homes near the Delaware River. That the dreaded yellow fever had found its way into the State House, the center of the United States government, was a frightening thought.

Soon after the discovery of Joseph Fry's corpse, everyone involved in the government fled the city of Philadelphia. Some sources say that his body was left to rot in his room and that it was not until the epidemic ended in November 1793 that whatever was left of Joseph Fry's remains was finally removed and buried in one of the many mass graves of yellow fever victims throughout the city, most likely in Washington Square just one block south.

The ghost of Joseph Fry continues to be seen by both staff and visitors at Independence Hall, and he seems to still be guarding this national historic landmark as vigilantly as he was when he tragically died of the yellow fever within its hallowed walls over two hundred years ago.

CHAPTER 5

WASHINGTON SQUARE'S
GHOSTLY GUARDIAN

Just one block south of Independence Hall you will encounter the lush 6.4-acre park now known as Washington Square. During the daytime, you will see numerous people picnicking on the many large, grassy areas underneath trees that have been standing for over two hundred years and others relaxing on benches, walking their dogs or watching their children play around the large fountain that stands in the center of the square. Far less crowded than its more popular sister park, Rittenhouse Square, Washington Square is a beautiful place to spend a peaceful afternoon in the Old City historic district of Philadelphia.

At night, however, Washington Square feels different. Once the sun sets and most people have gone back to their homes or hotels, walking through the park underneath its ancient, twisted trees can become an eerie experience. You might begin to feel that you're being followed, turning around to see no one there but still sensing that someone or something is watching you. You may begin to see things out of the corner of your eye—a shadow moving beside a tree, a dark figure standing alone on the grass. You blink, and they are gone. I have known people who tried to stay in Washington Square all night to see what they would experience, and none of them ever made it until sunrise. Because Washington Square is, in fact, a cemetery where thousands are buried in unmarked graves, and like many old graveyards, it is haunted by the spirits of its dead.

This piece of ground has existed as a public green space in Philadelphia since the city's inception. It was designated as Southeast Square in William

Penn's original 1682 plans for the city, his "green country town." For much of its early existence, Southeast Square was bisected by two creeks that were teeming with fish. It wasn't until approximately 1787 that the creeks were filled in, creating the uniform piece of land as we know it today.

For a period of exactly ninety years, from 1704 to 1794, Southeast Square was used as a cemetery—more accurately, a potter's field sometimes called the Strangers Burying Ground. In his comprehensive 1845 book *Annals of Philadelphia*, author John Fanning Watson described the genesis of the dead being laid to rest in what is now known as Washington Square:

> *In the center of the square was an enclosed ground, having a brick wall of about forty feet square, in which had been interred members of Joshua Carpenter's and the Story families, caused by the circumstance of a female of the former family having been interred there for suicide—a circumstance which excluded her from burial in the common church grounds of the city. There was an apple tree in the center, under which Mr. Carpenter was buried.*

The name of the Carpenter woman who took her own life is not recorded in any historical records that survive. But she was the first of many thousands who would eventually call Washington Square their grave; she is buried underneath where the beautiful fountain is today.

Southeast Square was also a hugely important meeting place for the enslaved and free Black men, women and children who lived in Philadelphia during the colonial era. Although Washington Square today has a few pieces of signage that nod to this history, I don't think it is talked about nearly enough, and it should be more widely known by the public. George W. Boudreau writes about this in his book *Independence: A Guide to Historic Philadelphia*:

> *Slaves had no private spaces they could consider their own. And outside of the private realm, they had no public spaces where they could join together for common interests. If allowed to attend church, they went to the master's house of worship where they would be consigned to the loft or balcony, subject to the many watchful eyes of the whites seated below. Any large gathering of slaves, or slaves and free blacks, was considered dangerous by Philadelphia's white leadership and was quickly dispersed. It is for this reason that a place like Washington Square became so important to Philadelphia's African Americans early on. Whites denied them burial in*

Washington Square. *Photo by Ii2nmd. Wikimedia Commons.*

the town's churchyards, but when the Strangers Burying Ground became the
final resting place of their friends and relatives, the space took on a symbolic
meaning in the minds of colonial Philadelphia's black community.

Indeed, the area around Washington Square, which was then considered the outskirts of the city, became one of Philadelphia's first Black neighborhoods. By the time of the American Revolution, Philadelphia's population included at least one thousand enslaved Africans and over one hundred Black people who were free. These are the people who built their own houses surrounding Washington Square, which was not only a place for mourning and remembering their dead but also a place of great celebration where they could openly honor their African heritage. Watson provides a snapshot of these practices in his 1845 *Annals of Philadelphia*:

It was the custom for the slave blacks, at the time of fairs and other great
holidays, to go there in the number of one thousand, of both sexes, and hold
their dances, dancing after the manner of their several nations in Africa,
and speaking and singing in their native dialects, thus cheerily amusing

themselves over the sleeping dust below! An aged lady, Mrs. H.S., has told me that she has often seen the Guinea negroes, in the days of her youth, going to the graves of their friends early in the morning, and there leaving them victuals and rum!

The American Revolution brought many more of the dead to Washington Square. Beginning in 1776, mass graves began to be dug that were twenty feet by thirty feet, and coffins containing soldiers who had died of disease were piled into these deep trenches until they were full, and then more mass graves had to be created. John Adams wrote in a letter dated April 13, 1777:

I have spent an hour this morning in the Congregation of the dead. I took a walk into the "Potter's Field," a burying ground between the new stone prison and the hospital, and I never in my whole life was affected with so much melancholy. The graves of the soldiers, who have been buried, in this ground…during the course of last summer, fall and winter, dead of the smallpox and camp diseases, are enough to make the heart of stone to melt away! The sexton told me that upwards of two thousand soldiers had been buried there, and by the appearance of the grave and trenches, it is most probable to me that he speaks within bounds.

Soldiers from the Revolution were not the only bodies interred in open mass graves at Washington Square during this time. While the British occupied Philadelphia in 1777, they turned the Walnut Street Jail, across the street from the square, into a place of misery and horror for all those unlucky enough to be placed within its walls. One man who was lucky enough to survive, named Jacob Ritter, said that the British would go days without feeding the prisoners, and so they were forced to eat leather and the roots of grass, and live rats were regarded as a delicacy. The British guards also beat the prisoners unmercifully. During the winter, broken windows allowed snow and freezing air to infiltrate the cells, causing many prisoners to die of hypothermia, disease and starvation. Jacob Ritter recalled that at least a dozen inmates at the Walnut Street Jail died every single day over the course of many months, and then their bodies were carried across the street and thrown into open mass graves in Washington Square, causing the area to be infested with the sickening odor of decomposing human flesh.

The yellow fever epidemic of 1793 decimated the population of Philadelphia, killing approximately five thousand citizens over a period of a few short months. Washington Square again was used for mass graves

Tomb of the Unknown Soldier of the American Revolution in Washington Square. *Photo by Ken Thomas. Wikimedia Commons.*

of those who had succumbed to the deadly fever. In 1794, the Stranger's Burying Ground was closed, since after ninety years and many mass burials, there was simply no room for any more bodies to be interred. In 1825, Southeast Square was renamed Washington Square, and an effort was made to beautify the space by planting over sixty different varieties of trees, many of which are still standing proudly today in the twenty-first century.

In 1954, it was decided to create a memorial for the two thousand unknown soldiers from the American Revolution buried in Washington Square. Two years later, in 1956, a team of archaeologists began digging. The first bodies found were those from the potter's field, noted because they were buried wrapped in canvas and not in coffins. Finally, one coffin was found that contained the body of a young man with a hole in his skull that suggested a bullet wound. This was the corpse that became entombed in the memorial where an eternal flame now burns. The irony is that there was no way to determine whether the soldier was British or American. Nevertheless, the memorial stands, and above a statue of George Washington, there is a moving inscription etched into the stone: "Freedom is a light for which many men have died in darkness," and then: "In unmarked graves within this square lie thousands of unknown soldiers of Washington's Army who died of wounds and sickness during the Revolutionary War."

The dead are not quiet in Washington Square. The reasons why go back to the eighteenth century, because during the years that the dead were being laid to rest in the square, there was an epidemic of grave robbing. This was done by "the resurrectionists," who would come to the grounds in the gloom of the night, digging up those who had been freshly buried and selling their corpses to the highest bidder. Those who purchased these illegally acquired bodies were mostly doctors and medical students, who used them to study human anatomy and improve medical practices, as Philadelphia was the leader in medical science well into the nineteenth century. Two of the most famous physicians in colonial Philadelphia, Dr. Benjamin Rush and Dr. Philip Syng Physick, were both known to acquire dead bodies in this manner. Author Thomas H. Keels relates a piece of macabre history about both men and their personal connections with the exhumation of the dead:

> The city's most notorious resurrectionist showed up at Physick's door late at night the same day Rush was buried. He asked Physick if the good doctor wanted Benjamin Rush. When Physick, confused, stammered that Dr. Rush had been buried that day, the graverobber replied, "I know. For $20 I can have him on your dissecting table first thing tomorrow." Physick said no and slammed the door. But the encounter so unnerved him that he left detailed instructions on how his body was to be treated when he died a quarter-century later: No autopsy or post-mortem, regardless of the circumstances of his death. The only two people allowed to handle his body were two elderly female servants who had been with his family for decades. Once they had finished washing and laying him out, they were to cocoon his body in layers of blankets and leave it in his bed, with a roaring fire in the hearth day and night, until he had reached such a stage of putrefaction that even the most desperate graverobber wouldn't look at him twice. Only then would his remains be buried at Christ Church Burial Ground. But even then, the coffin was to be sealed, and a guard posted over his grave for several weeks to make sure the bodysnatchers didn't snatch him.

It is also a known historical fact that the grave robbers would often specifically target the bodies of Black men, women and children who were buried in Washington Square. The spiritual leaders of the African American community were outraged. Richard Allen, who was born into slavery in Delaware and rose to be anointed a bishop, and Absalom Jones, also born into slavery in Sussex County, Delaware, and who later became the first Black priest ordained in the Episcopal Church, together formed the Free African Society in 1787 at the same time the United States Constitution was being written. These great men founded two of the first Black congregations in the United States, the African Methodist Episcopal Church (Mother Bethel) and the African Episcopal Church of St. Thomas, respectively, both of which are still active today.

Richard Allen and Absalom Jones repeatedly asked the government of Philadelphia to build a protective wall around the area of Washington Square where the Black community buried their dead, but their pleas were ignored. Thus, it fell to ordinary citizens to guard the dead against grave robbing, and that is where stories about the haunting of Washington Square begin.

John Fanning Watson writes of the origins of the haunting in his 1845 *Annals of Philadelphia*:

> *Some of my contemporaries will remember the simple-hearted innocent Leah, a half-crazed, specter-looking, elderly maiden lady, tall and thin, of the Society of Friends. Among her oddities, she sometimes used to pass the night, wrapped in a blanket, between the graves at this place, for the avowed purpose of frightening away the doctors!*

I must admit, I was taken aback when I first read this passage in research for this book. Every telling of the ghost stories of Washington Square, including how I have always told this story for the Ghost Tour of Philadelphia, speaks of Leah as a legendary, almost mythic figure shrouded in mystery. But it is apparent from the way John Fanning Watson wrote this passage in 1845 that Leah was indeed a real person whom he and others of his age personally knew. This eccentric, "half-crazed, specter-looking," elderly Quaker woman, it seems, did become a real specter after her death. Stories have been handed down through time that Leah died in Washington Square itself, and her frail body was discovered in the early morning light lying down on someone's freshly covered grave, passing away in her sleep as she protected the body below from prying fingers.

Although many spirits have been witnessed in Washington Square over the years, including those of Revolutionary War soldiers in tattered uniforms and bloodstained yellow fever victims, the ghost of Leah is the one seen most often. She guarded the dead here in life, and it seems that her own death was not enough to stop her mission. Those who walk through Washington Square at night have often glimpsed the solitary figure of a tall old woman, stooped over with age, wearing a long black dress and a long black hooded cloak, a frayed blanket around her shoulders. She is most frequently seen in the vicinity of the Tomb of the Unknown Solider in Washington Square, and often appears in photographs that are taken at that location.

Perhaps the most chilling encounter with the ghost of Leah was experienced by a Philadelphia police detective in the 1990s. This detective, under the condition of anonymity, told their story directly to author Charles J. Adams III for his 1998 book *Philadelphia Ghost Stories*:

> *I was walking through Washington Square on a rather cold November morning, as I did quite often from my house on South 6th to the Round House* [Philly's police headquarters]. *I stopped for a few minutes to pour some coffee from a plastic cup into my insulated jug, and out over toward Walnut Street I saw an old woman rustling through the leaves. It really wasn't anything unusual, I figured it was just* [a homeless woman] *wandering through the park. But something looked odd about* [her]. *She seemed somehow out of place. I mean, there was something about her that didn't look right. Maybe it was the cop in me, but I walked closer.*
>
> *Here's where it gets weird. I looked closely at her and the more I tried to get a make on her face, the more trouble I had seeing any face. Honest to God, it was if there was no face, no head, under the blanket that was wrapped over her shoulders! I tried not to be noticeable to her. I kept my distance and kind of staked her out. But the strangest thing was yet to come. You're going to think I'm some sort of whacko when I tell you what happened next, and you'll also know why I don't want any of my friends or any bigwigs on the force to know who's talking here....But I'll swear on a stack of bibles that as I watched that old lady, she just up and disappeared....Vanished—right before my eyes. Now, I've seen a lot of strange things in my days, but this was the strangest. I stood there like I had been punched in the face. That woman, or whatever, just flat out disappeared!*

What makes this account so valuable is that the witness had no knowledge of Leah or of Washington Square's hauntings before having this experience and relating their tale to the author of *Philadelphia Ghost Stories*. After the detective shared their story, Charles J. Adams III then told the detective the legends of Leah. After hearing that, the detective said to Adams:

I never believed in ghosts before, but with what I saw and what you just told me, maybe there's something to it. All I know is that whenever I walk through the square—and I do quite often—I keep looking for the same woman or…whatever. I never saw her after that one time…and maybe I don't really want to.

Even today, the bones of those long dead sometimes still find their way to the surface in Washington Square. The next time you walk through this place, especially at night, make sure you walk with respect, for with every step you take, you are walking on someone's body. Remember them as you pass through the square in the darkness, and keep your eyes open. You never know—you might be added to the long list of those who have encountered the faceless phantom of Leah, guarding the thousands of dead in Washington Square for all eternity.

CHAPTER 6

SEAFARING SPECTERS ON THE USS *OLYMPIA*

There is an old superstition that says ghosts cannot cross water. If that superstition is true, what happens to the spirits of those whose lives end on a ship while at sea—do their souls remain trapped there forever? Throughout the world, there are many ships that are reported to be haunted, and one of the most historically significant "ghost ships" of them all is the USS *Olympia*. It has been resting quietly in Philadelphia since 1922 and has been open for tours at the Independence Seaport Museum on the Delaware River since 1996. The oldest steel warship in the entire world that is still afloat, as well as the only surviving naval vessel of her era, the USS *Olympia* is one of the city's most priceless historic landmarks—and one of its most unique and unsettling haunted places, with at least nineteen deaths recorded onboard. These deaths mostly did not occur in battle but by murder, suicide, accidents and disease. The ship is wonderful to visit during the day, but walking the decks of the *Olympia* can be terrifying at night.

The *Olympia* was built in San Francisco 1892 and began its illustrious career in 1895 and was, at the time, one of the fastest ships in the world. The USS *Olympia* is 344 feet long and carried a crew of up to 450 enlisted men. Her crew was notably diverse due to the high rate of immigration to the United States during the nineteenth century. In 1898, sailors aboard the *Olympia* hailed from places such as China, England, Mexico, Austria, Italy, Ireland, Russia and Turkey. However, at this time, the navy had a rule requiring all crew members to speak only English during their working hours. Officers had their own separate area of the ship to live in, with their own personal (but still small) quarters. The regular crew all slept in hammocks that were

The USS *Olympia* in 1902. *Courtesy of the U.S. Navy.*

hung extremely close together, with zero privacy or personal space. At this time, a typical period of enlistment was three years, and for those three years, sailors would rarely leave the USS *Olympia*. It became their entire world, a "floating city," as some historians have called it. Crew members set up their own businesses tattooing, cutting hair, selling ice cream and making illicit alcohol, and there was even an amateur dance academy. The floors of the ship were, and are, painted a deep red—to make the human blood spilled during battles less noticeable.

From almost the very beginning of its existence, crew members whispered about the USS *Olympia* being cursed, or "hoodooed." An article that appeared in the January 1896 issue of the *Anglo-Jingoist* newspaper related the many tragic events that unfolded in 1895, the first year the ship was active:

> *Some of the sailors on the cruiser, are so well satisfied that she is hoodooed, that nothing short of a miracle can change their belief. Once in a while she seems to escape from the baleful influence of the hoodoo; but just when the people are congratulating themselves on the new turn of affairs, she falls into another streak of bad luck and disgrace.*
> *April 24, 1895—John Johnson killed in gun drill*
> *April 26—Seaman's leg removed in anchor accident*

May 27—Three seamen overcome by noxious boiler fumes
June—Four discharged shipmates die returning home
June 26—Fire in the drum room
August 29—Cholera outbreak in Honolulu. Quarantined, no liberty
October 26—Fought fire in bunkers for nine days as the ship fought a
typhoon almost losing men at sea
January 21, 1896—Olympia disgraced, loses race with the steamer
Empress of India.

The first tragedy that occurred aboard the USS *Olympia* on April 24, 1895, is one that made a lasting impact on the vessel, perhaps creating its first ghost. A horrific accident occurred when a man named John N. Johnson went to test-fire one of the ship's massive guns for the first time. Unfortunately, this particular gun was not properly mounted, and when Johnson fired it, the heavy gun was projected backward, brutally crushing him to death on the deck in front of his fellow crew members and friends. The details of the sudden and horrific death of gunner John N. Johnson were recorded by a crew member named Louis Stanley Young:

*John N. Johnson, captain of gun number three, stepped to his place to fire,
with a joke to the gun's crew and a smile on his lip. The next instant, with
the smile still lingering on his face, he was hurled into eternity. The great
gun recoiled off its carriage, snapping like pipe stems the massive steel bolts
that held it in place, crashed down on poor Johnson, hurling him to the deck
and killing him almost instantly.*

John N. Johnson's tragic demise deeply affected the brand-new crew of the USS *Olympia*, some of whom openly wept. One of them made a drawing of the gruesome scene, and yet another wrote a poem commemorating the terrible event:

No chance for a prayer,
Not a word of farewell,
To his shipmates around
That loved him so well…
His frame, crushed and quivering,
Was borne to the deck;
"No hope," said our surgeon,
"It has broken his neck."

The location of John N. Johnson's tragic death.

In May 1896, the USS *Olympia* was responsible for the heroic rescue of thirty-eight men from another sinking ship. While this was one of the first of many instances of the heroism of the ship's crew, one sailor named Lou Tisdale described the grim reality of the situation:

> *For a time, the water was black with human beings. When we had hauled as many into our boats as they would hold, others struggling for life would cling to our gunwales and to our oars and would have swamped us had we not resorted to the inhumanity of breaking the already benumbed fingers, thus forcing them to relax their last grip on life. In my boat one man died after we had taken him in. He was thrown overboard, and another picked up in his place.*

The following year, in December 1897, a Black crew member of the USS *Olympia* named Frank Epps was murdered while the ship was docked near Nagasaki, Japan. This became a large scandal that ended up being investigated by Congress and even commented on by President William McKinley. Soon after the tragedy occurred, Captain Charles Vernon Gridley wrote the following account to the Secretary of the Navy:

> *Sir: I regret to inform the Department of the death and probable murder of Frank Epps, apprentice, first class, of this vessel, under the following circumstances. Epps had been granted liberty from 1pm December 12 to 7am December 13. He was with companies ashore until 8pm of the 12th,*

when he left in a sampan and started for the Olympia. From testimony of several of the crew of the British skip Saint Enoch, they saw three men scuffling in the sampan about 8:15pm that night, and then cries for help. They also saw one of the men struck at with a stick of some kind, and then pushed or thrown overboard. They sent a sampan to his assistance, but by the time they reached the spot all was quiet, and the sampan in which the row had occurred had put out its light and was hurrying away so fast that they could not overtake it, but they succeeded in picking up a cap with Epps's name on it. Ship's boats were sent out to drag for the body, which was recovered yesterday afternoon by a Japanese, who was dragging in the company with our boats. The body was found to have a wound over the left eye. A board of inquest, assembled by order of the commander in chief, opinioned that Epps had been murdered by person or persons unknown by being pushed overboard out of a sampan, having been previously struck by a blow of sufficient force to produce insensibility....Epps was buried this afternoon at Urakami Cemetery, about 3 miles from Nagasaki, with appropriate naval honors, and a headstone is to be erected by his shipmates.

According to witness testimony, the last words of Frank Epps were, "Help! Oh God!" On January 11, 1898, two Japanese men were convicted of the murder of Frank Epps and sentenced to each pay a fine of 150 yen—and were then allowed to go free. Many people believed this to be a miscarriage of justice. The exact motive for the killing of Frank Epps was never clearly determined. Because he was buried so far from home and died so near the USS *Olympia*, there are many who believe that Epps became another one of the ship's restless spirits after his violent demise.

The USS *Olympia* secured her place in history with the Battle of Manila Bay in the Philippines on May 1, 1898, which proved to be the decisive battle of the Spanish-American War. At this time, the *Olympia* was led by Commodore George Dewey, who had first entered naval service during the Civil War. At approximately 5:40 a.m. on May 1, 1898, the USS *Olympia* stood ready to face the Spanish fleet, and Dewey gave his immortal order to Captain Charles Vernon Gridley, who was stationed in the ship's conning tower: "You may fire when you are ready, Gridley." Although the battle was ferocious, Commodore Dewey never moved from his position on the *Olympia*'s top deck, which is now commemorated by brass footprints. By early afternoon, the Battle of Manila Bay was over, with the United States achieving an overwhelming victory over Spanish forces. The historical impact of the USS *Olympia*'s success in this battle cannot be overstated. The

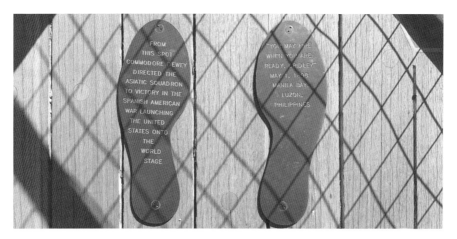

Where Commodore George Dewey stood during the Battle of Manila Bay.

United States, 122 years after declaring its independence from England, now established itself as a global superpower in the eyes of the entire world. For his service, George Dewey was given the title of Admiral of the Navy; to this day, he remains the only officer to hold it.

For the *Olympia*'s captain, Charles Vernon Gridley, the Battle of Manila Bay was the crowning and final triumph of his long and illustrious career. He was, by the time of the battle, seriously ill with dysentery and undiagnosed liver cancer. Dewey offered to relieve Gridley of his command, but Gridley refused and never left his post in the conning tower during the entire battle. However, after it was over, he was so ill he had to be carried back to the captain's quarters. Charles Vernon Gridley was sent home later that month, on May 25, 1895. He knew he was nearing the end of his life, writing, "I think I am done for it, personally." One of the *Olympia*'s crew members wrote of Gridley's final poignant moments aboard the vessel:

> *He came up out of his cabin dressed in civilian clothes and was met by the rear admiral [Dewey] who extended him a most cordial hand. A look of troubled disappointment flitted across the captain's brow, but vanished when he stepped to the head of the gangway and, looking over, saw, not the launch, but a twelve-oared cutter manned entirely by officers of the Olympia. There were men in the boat who had not pulled a stroke for a quarter of a century. Old Glory was at the stern and a captain's silken coach-whip at the bow; and when Captain Gridley, beloved alike by officers and men, entered the boat, it was up oars, and all that, just as though they*

One of the senior officers' staterooms.

were common sailors who were to row him over.…When he sat down upon the handsome boat-cloth that was spread for him, he bowed his head, and his hands hid his face as First-Lieutenant Reese, acting coxswain, ordered, "Shove off; out oars; give away!" Later in the day the lookout on the bridge reported, "Zafiro under way sir," and the deck officer passed on the word until a little twitter from Pat Murray's pipe brought all the other bo's'ns around him, and in concert they sang out, "Stand by to man the rigging!" Not the Olympia alone, but every other ship in the squadron dressed and manned, and the last we ever saw of our dear captain he was sitting on a chair…listening to the [Olympia's] old band play.

This was a fitting and deeply moving tribute to a man who had given his life to service in the U.S. Navy. Captain Charles Vernon Gridley never made it home. He died on June 5, 1898, while on board a ship near Japan, a little over a month after his final heroic acts during the Battle of Manila Bay. He is buried in the Lakeside Cemetery of Erie, Pennsylvania. However, many believe his spirit may still be found roaming the captain's quarters of the ship he loved, his last command, the USS *Olympia.*

AT THE TURN OF the twentieth century, two more deaths occurred onboard the USS *Olympia* that have left ghostly echoes that continue to the present day. In 1902, two men committed suicide in the officer's quarters within five days of each other. The first to die was Chaplain William F. Morrison, on September 10, 1902. Morrison had been a naval chaplain since 1881 and had begun working on the *Olympia* in March 1902. An article in the *Boston Daily Globe* newspaper reported that the Reverend Morrison was suffering from a bout of "mental depression" and that he had suffered a similar condition ten or twelve years earlier. On September 10, Morrison stepped outside of his stateroom in "Officer's Country," sat down in a chair, placed a loaded revolver in his mouth and took his own life. He was fifty-two years old.

Five days later, on September 15, 1902, Lieutenant John R. Morris killed himself inside of his stateroom, also by placing his service revolver in his mouth and pulling the trigger. He was about thirty years old and unmarried. The *Boston Daily Globe* reported that the USS *Olympia*'s crew was in a state of shock and gloom over these two deaths. One crew member was quoted as saying, "This ship will be known as 'the suicide ship' if these awful deeds keep on." The newspaper also noted that among the crew, "superstitions were rife." As far as why Lieutenant John Morris chose to take his own life, it was speculated in the newspapers that his experience with the tragedy aboard the USS *Maine* may have been a factor:

> *He was on several ships before being assigned to the Maine, upon which he was when it was blown up in Havana harbor. Lieutenant Morris was sitting conversing just abaft of the after turret when the explosions occurred. He was thrown heavily to the deck, and later, in endeavoring to reach the side and his station for the boats in abandoning the ship*

A view of the berth deck.

he was repeatedly knocked down by flying wreckage and debris. Some think that like many other officers and men of the Maine who escaped, Lieutenant Morris never recovered from the awful shock and effects of that momentous disaster.

Over the years, visitors and staff have seen the figure of a man standing in one of the staterooms of Officer's Country, a man who then vanishes. Whether this is the ghost of the Reverend William Morrison or Lieutenant John Morris is not known, but several paranormal investigation teams have captured EVP (electronic voice phenomena) recordings in the area where both men met their melancholy deaths, hearing the words "Help me," and "God, God, God."

DURING WORLD WAR I, the USS *Olympia* patrolled up and down the East Coast looking out for German U-boats. In October 1921, the ship carried out her final mission: transporting the remains of the Unknown Soldier from Le Havre, France, to Arlington National Cemetery in Washington, D.C. The soldier's coffin would not fit through the hatches belowdecks, so it was wrapped in canvas on the topside deck with a twenty-four-hour honor guard. The bad luck of the *Olympia* carried on to the last, as the ship's journey was wracked by encounters with both a tropical cyclone and the 1921 Tampa Bay hurricane. Many feared that the ship would capsize, and it came perilously close to doing so several times, with thirty-foot waves coming up as high as the bridge and flooding the ship. The Unknown Soldier's casket was lashed down tightly to the deck. Through it all, the honor guard remained on deck with the body of the Unknown Soldier. One of the guards, Frederick A. Landry, said,

I began feeling sorry for myself, having to stand there in such a small area with the rain and wind pelting me in the face, but my self-sorry didn't last long. I soon realized that what I was doing was little enough compared to what the Unknown Soldier had done—given his life.

The USS *Olympia* made it through the storms without any loss of crew and finally arrived in Washington, D.C., with the body of the Unknown Soldier. The ship's chaplain, the Reverend Edward A. Duff, was quoted as saying, "God was with the ship, and He was watching over the crew because a grateful nation was awaiting the ship that carried the Unknown Soldier."

Stairs down to the engine room.

Following the successful completion of this task, the USS *Olympia* was decommissioned in 1922, after twenty-seven years of remarkable service in the United States Navy.

ON OCTOBER 29, 2010, the *Philadelphia Inquirer* published an article by Edward Colimore titled, "Some Say They've Seen Ghosts on the USS Olympia," which included interviews with several people who had experienced frightening paranormal activity aboard the vessel. Among the most haunted areas of the ship are the engine room and boiler room, where mysterious voices and footsteps have been heard. A longtime volunteer named Harry Burkhardt said that while working down in the boiler room, "I felt two hands grab my arms—and they were icy cold." He quickly turned around, only to find there no one there. Burkhardt and another employee also saw "a dark form dart across a doorway," which terrified them. A paranormal investigator named Melissa Miller saw the full-body apparition of a man appear in the engine room, which is likely the ghost of a former sailor who fell forty feet to his death in that location. With her tape recorder rolling, she asked, "Is there someone here?" She heard nothing, but reviewing the recording later, she heard the voice of a man answer her on the tape, saying, "I think I'm in love."

Miller also saw another ghost in the area of the *Olympia* where the crew slept: "It came out of a corridor, turned right, walked to the rear of the ship, and dissipated into the darkness. I could see what he was wearing—boots, slacks, a button-down shirt, and short-brimmed hat." Harry Burkhardt also participated in an EVP session on board. While sitting on the berth deck, he asked, "Do you mind us being here?" Replaying the recording, he heard a man screaming, "*Get out!*" On the topside deck, a visitor was taking photographs when she noticed a man in a white navy uniform standing in the pilot house, holding the wheel. Some have wondered if this could be the spirit of Commodore George Dewey, reliving the triumph of the Battle of Manila Bay.

The television series *Ghost Hunters* investigated the USS *Olympia* in an episode of its seventh season in 2011, and investigators heard footsteps coming from the exact location where John N. Johnson was crushed to death in 1895, followed by a door loudly slamming shut. For several years, the Ghost Tour of Philadelphia also conducted a ghost tour of the USS *Olympia* during the month of October. I was one of the guides who led that tour, and I had an experience the very first night I did it. The shipkeepers of the *Olympia* went above and beyond to make the experience atmospheric for guests, turning off most of the electric lights onboard and placing lanterns throughout the decks. At the end of the first ghost tour, I was standing on the main deck as the guests left the ship. I turned and looked toward the galley, and I saw the figure of a man quickly walk out of the kitchen (which is impossible to do because of a metal gate) across the deck and then disappear. He was transparent, he walked extremely fast and I couldn't see anything of him below the knees. It happened in two or three seconds. I froze and then realized that to get back to the staff office

Where I saw a ghost emerge from the kitchen on the left.

where I'd left my belongings, I had no choice but to walk directly past the galley where I had just seen the man. I made it off the *Olympia* in record time that night.

History remains vividly present onboard the USS *Olympia*, which is truly one of Philadelphia's treasures. The Independence Seaport Museum is raising funds to continue the preservation of the ship, which badly needs to be dry-docked so its deteriorating hull may be fully repaired. I highly recommend you visit the *Olympia* and take a step backward in time. You never know; one of the many specters from her extraordinary past might just reach out and touch you.

CHAPTER 7

EERIE ECHOES AT
EASTERN STATE PENITENTIARY

Wandering through the neighborhood of Fairmount, not far from the Philadelphia Museum of Art, you may be surprised to encounter what looks like a gigantic medieval Gothic castle standing ominously among the rowhomes and restaurants. This is Eastern State Penitentiary, one of Philadelphia's most iconic historic sites. Construction on the prison began two hundred years ago in 1821, and it received its first prisoner, a Black farmer named Charles Williams sentenced to two years for theft, in 1829. From the beginning of its existence, Eastern State Penitentiary was a notable tourist attraction. When Charles Dickens visited the United States in 1842, he declared that the two places he most wanted to see were Niagara Falls and the new prison in Philadelphia, whose design eventually inspired three hundred other correctional institutions throughout the world. Closed in 1971, the prison was then abandoned for twenty years before reopening as a museum categorized as a "stabilized ruin." Eastern State still inspires people to enter its gate and explore the crumbling world of beautifully preserved decay within its high stone walls. Its fascinating history and fearful appearance inspire passion and curiosity, but there is another reason why people are drawn to this national historic landmark. It is said to be one of the most haunted places in the nation, and perhaps the world.

> *Let the avenue to this house be rendered difficult and gloomy by mountains and morasses. Let its doors be of iron. Let the grating occasion by the opening and shutting of them be increased by an echo that shall deeply pierce the soul. —Dr. Benjamin Rush*

Dr. Rush was one of several prominent citizens, including Benjamin Franklin and Bishop William White, who founded the Philadelphia Society for Alleviating the Miseries of Public Prisons in 1787, the same year as the writing of the United States Constitution. They created this organization as a response to the horrific conditions at the Walnut Street Jail, which at the time was merely a place to house criminals, not reform them. Prisoners at the Walnut Street Jail were often kept in filthy rooms with no separation of men, women and children. Crime and violence among the prisoners were commonplace, aided and abetted by the prison guards, who would charge the inmates money for items such as clothing, a bed, food and alcohol. Disease, especially typhoid or "jail fever," was rampant, and many who ended up in the Walnut Street Jail returned there again and again after committing further crimes. It was clear that something had to be done, and what the society came up with was an idea never before attempted. Instead of a jail, they would build a "penitentiary," a place where those who broke the law would be encouraged to look within themselves and repent for their sins, hopefully emerging as better human beings.

The site chosen for what would become Eastern State Penitentiary was located on a hill on the outskirts of Philadelphia that had previously been a cherry orchard. This is why many people early in the prison's history often referred to it as Cherry Hill. To decide who would design this innovative structure, the society held a contest and chose a young architect named John Haviland. The outer walls of the penitentiary were constructed first, intentionally echoing the façade of a horrific medieval fortress in order to strike fear into both the prisoners entering it as well as the general public, as a deterrent to crime. All in the city below could look up and see exactly where they would go if they broke the law. The walls are thirty feet high and continue ten feet below the ground to deter escapees, although some did manage to get over or under them throughout the prison's history, as we will later see. The battlements of the towers and the slit windows on the exterior are for show—if you were to stand on the battlements, the stone would only come up to your knees, and the castle-like windows are not visible from the interior.

Within these Gothic walls, Haviland created a design with seven single-story cellblocks radiating outward from a central hub. This way, guards in the center rotunda would be able to simply turn around and have a clear view of every single cellblock. This was an essential aspect of the plan, because Eastern State Penitentiary was to be administered under what became known worldwide as the Pennsylvania System, or separate system.

The exterior of Eastern State Penitentiary. Photo by Carol M. Highsmith. *Courtesy of the Library of Congress.*

To encourage repentance, the cellblocks were built with high vaulted ceilings to give the feel of a church. In his book *Eastern State Penitentiary: Crucible of Good Intentions*, author Norman Johnston writes:

> *As inmates were to serve their entire sentence in their cells, these cells were generously proportioned by nineteenth century and even late twentieth century standards. The thirty-eight cells in block one, the first constructed, were eight by twelve feet and had brick vaults ten feet high at the crown. An iron latticework door and a solid wooden door connected each cell to an individual exercise yard the same width as the cell and eighteen feet long. Initially there were no doors from the corridor to the individual cells; access to the cell was only through outside the iron door in the wall of each inmate's exercise yard. There were, however, rectangular openings in the corridor wall through which food and work materials could be passed.... Haviland decided against the customary toilet buckets and instead designed a rudimentary flush toilet for each cell.*

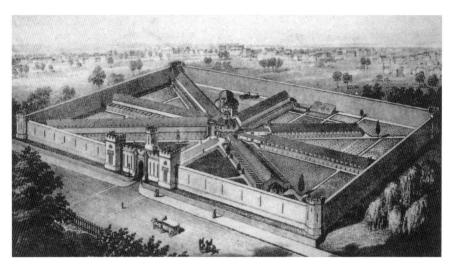

Eastern State Penitentiary in 1855. Lithograph by Duval and Company. *Wikimedia Commons.*

Thus, Eastern State Penitentiary contained indoor plumbing for all its inmates before the White House did. The cells were lit by a single narrow skylight known as the "dead eye" or the "eye of God." Upon arrival at the prison, new inmates would be assigned a number and then hooded and led to the cell where they would serve out their sentence. Inmates were hooded both to prevent them from knowing the layout of the prison and to help preserve their anonymity so they would, in theory at least, have a better chance at a successful reintegration into the outside after their release. Prisoners were not allowed to see or communicate with one another in any way, although nearly from the beginning ways were found around this rule, including by tapping in code on the sewer pipes, which had to be redesigned several times to stop this.

For the first several days of their confinement, inmates were left to themselves. After this, they could request a Bible to read and some kind of basic work to do to pass the time, such as woodwork or shoemaking. They were not allowed any visits or letters from family or friends for the duration of their confinement or even a newspaper. For as long as they were incarcerated at Eastern State, prisoners would have no communication or news from the outside world. However, they were not fully deprived of human contact. The warden was required to speak with each inmate every single day, and religious instructors could also be summoned for spiritual guidance. Guards wore socks over their shoes so they could move about the cellblocks without being heard, and even the wheels of the feeding carts were covered in leather to preserve the monk-like silence of the prison, encouraging inmates to look deep within their own souls. It is also important to note that from the very beginning, and for most of its history, an overwhelming majority of the inmate population at Eastern State Penitentiary, both men and women, was Black.

Like the city of Philadelphia itself, the separate system at Eastern State Penitentiary was an experiment, and many throughout the nation and the world wondered if it would succeed or fail. The first report from an outside source came in 1833 with the book *On the Penitentiary System in the United States*, written by Gustave de Beaumont and Alexis de Tocqueville, who had visited Eastern State in 1831 and interviewed several inmates who were incarcerated there. One of them was John Wilson, who had been sentenced to ten years for robbery. Wilson had been in the Walnut Street Jail three times; Eastern State was his fourth:

> *If they had put me here for my first crime....I never should have committed a second; but one always leaves Walnut Street* [Jail] *worse than when he enters it. Nowhere but here, is it possible to reflect....During the first two months I was near falling into despair. But reading and labor have gradually comforted me.*

Not all inmates reacted well to the separate system. Another man interviewed by Beaumont and Tocqueville said, "I do not believe...that I

Re-creation of a prisoner's cell.

ever shall leave this cell alive; solitude is fatal to the human constitution; it will kill me." Charles Dickens, who was so eager to visit Eastern State Penitentiary in 1842, was repulsed and enraged by what he saw there, and he wrote extensively about his feelings in the subsequent book *American Notes for General Circulation*, believing that the separate system was inhumane and would only result in driving the inmates toward madness:

> *Looking down these dreary passages, the dull repose and quiet that prevails, is awful. Occasionally, there is a drowsy sound from some lone weaver's shuttle, or shoemaker's last, but it is stifled by the thick walls and heavy dungeon-door, and only serves to make the general stillness more profound. Over the head and face of every prisoner who comes into this melancholy house, a black hood is drawn; and in this dark shroud, an emblem of the curtain dropped between him and the living world, he is led to the cell from which he never again comes forth, until his whole term of imprisonment has expired....He is a man buried alive; to be dug out in the slow round of years....And though he lives to be in the same cell ten weary years, he has no means of knowing, down to the very last hour, in what part of the building it is situated; what kind of men there are about him; whether in the long winter night there are living people near, or he is in some lonely corner of the great jail, with walls, and passages, and iron doors between him and the nearest sharer in its solitary horrors....I hold this slow and daily tampering with the mysteries of the brain to be immeasurably worse than any torture of the body.*

Although Eastern State Penitentiary was designed to reform its inmates, there were punishments administered to those who broke the rules. For a first infraction, one of the daily meals could be withheld, but for more serious offenses, prisoners were subjected to methods which can fairly be described as torture. Inmates could be confined indefinitely to "dark cells" in which the skylight had been covered and fed with meager rations of bread and water. A prisoner named Seneca Plimly was punished by being stripped to the waist and tied to the wall of his exercise yard. Then guards poured a dozen buckets of water over his head. It was December, so cold that the water froze to ice on his naked skin and icicles hung from his hair. There was also a device some believe was created by none other than Dr. Benjamin Rush called "the tranquilizing chair" or "the mad chair," in which prisoners were strapped down so tightly that their limbs would turn black from lack of circulation. Finally, there was the iron gag. The gag was fitted onto the prisoner's tongue,

Top: A view of cellblock 7.

Bottom: The baseball diamond at Eastern State, with a view of the modern city beyond its walls.

and chains from the gag were linked to the prisoner's arms, which were crossed behind their back, so that even the slightest movement would begin tearing the tongue. An inmate by the name of Matthias Mecumpsey died at Eastern State while being subjected to the iron gag, but his cause of death was listed in the official records as "apoplexy."

By the time the first three cellblocks were completed, it was already clear that the penitentiary was in serious danger of becoming overcrowded. Architect John Haviland had to compromise his design so that each cellblock would consist of two stories instead of one. This meant that cellblocks 4 through 7 had a second floor that could not be seen by guards in the center rotunda and also that those cells did not have an outside exercise yard. At first, every other cell was left empty for exercise use by second-floor inmates, but as more and more prisoners came to the building, this began to be impossible. Ten years after it had opened, Eastern State Penitentiary had double the number of inmates it was constructed to house, an issue that became greater and greater as the years went by, eventually leading to the official abandonment of the separate system in 1913. By many accounts, it had effectively ended much earlier, during the 1860s, when it became necessary to begin having two inmates, and sometimes as many as four, share a single cell. The Pennsylvania system that Eastern State had been founded on ultimately failed because it became impossible to enforce. In the twentieth century, the penitentiary evolved into a maximum-security congregate prison like countless others where isolation was used as a harsh punishment instead of as a means of personal redemption, a complete and somewhat sad reversal from its original, idealistic intent.

LIFE INSIDE THE WALLS of Eastern State Penitentiary was not always grim. Although inmates were racially segregated until 1964, its new congregate model in the twentieth century allowed for a sense of community that had not been possible before. Inmates worked together, ate meals together and were allowed to play musical instruments; keep small pets such as birds, mice or cats; and decorate their cells. Several of the astonishingly beautiful murals painted by prisoners in their cells and the chaplain's office can still be seen to this day. For outdoor exercise, there was a basketball court, a weightlifting yard and a baseball diamond—at the far end of which there is still a metal fence perched on top of the stone outer walls to try to prevent home runs from flying into the surrounding neighborhood that by this time had grown up around the prison. However, baseball teams were always Whites against Blacks, which contributed to racial tensions among inmates and guards. There was a chapel constructed for Christian worship, and in 1923, a Jewish synagogue was created, the first ever built in a United States prison. It must also be stated that beginning in the late 1950s, Muslims repeatedly asked the administration for their own place of worship within the penitentiary walls, but their requests were always denied.

On August 8, 1929, Eastern State received its most famous inmate, Chicago mafia boss Al "Scarface" Capone. Sentenced to one year in prison for carrying a concealed weapon in Atlantic City, Capone spent eight months behind bars in Philadelphia, his first incarceration. The *Philadelphia Public*

Ledger newspaper suggested in an article published on August 20, 1929, that he lived in relative luxury at Eastern State Penitentiary:

> *"Yes, very comfortable," observed Al Capone yesterday with a smile as he glanced around his cell in the "Park Avenue" block of the Eastern Penitentiary. And the former leader of Chicago's racketeers wasn't exaggerating one bit the conditions under which he is an enforced guest of the Commonwealth of Pennsylvania. As he spoke the strains of a waltz were being emitted by a powerful cabinet radio receiver of handsome design and fine finish. The formerly cheerless floor of the cell was covered by a beautiful rug in which soft colors and luxurious textures were combined. On the once grim walls of the penal chamber hung tasteful paintings. The whole room was suffused in the glow of a desk lamp, which stood on a polished desk. Nearby was a chest of drawers and a bed. Everything was cheery and homelike.*

A second article published the following day in the *Philadelphia Record* newspaper suggests that the *Public Ledger* exaggerated the elements of Al Capone's cell. He shared the cell with another inmate, as was customary by this time, and the two men slept on plain cots. The rug on the floor was prison-made. There was a victrola, a vase of flowers and paintings on the walls, but these were not unusual sights for a prison cell at Eastern State during this time. However, some stories suggest that there was occasionally a third presence inside the cell. It was while at ESP that Al

The restored synagogue at Eastern State.

"Park Avenue" at ESP. Al Capone's cell was located on the bottom left.

Capone reportedly began to be haunted by the ghost of one of the men he had ordered killed in the Saint Valentine's Day Massacre, James Clark, whose real name had been Albert Kachellek. Capone would wake guards (and presumably his cellmate) up in the middle of the night screaming for "Jimmy" to leave him alone. Later, when he was imprisoned at Alcatraz, the haunting grew worse, and guards would frequently hear Al Capone having conversations with a man who was not physically present in the cell with him. Whether Capone was truly being haunted by the specter of James Clark or if it was a manifestation of the neurosyphilis that eventually led to his death, we will never know for sure.

In 1945, perhaps the most daring escape from Eastern State Penitentiary occurred. The mastermind behind this escape was a mason named Clarence Klinedinst, who was serving time at ESP for burglary and forgery. Transferred to a cell at the end of block 7 in 1944, he immediately began digging a tunnel that would take him and others out underneath the walls of the prison. Author Paul Kahan writes of the specifics of Klinedinst's impressive feat in his excellent book *Eastern State Penitentiary: A History*:

> *Klinedinst's tunnel was pretty sophisticated, given the conditions…. Klinedinst had made a seven foot ladder that led from his cell to the tunnel, wooden boards to shore up the tunnels walls and a string of electric lights throughout….There's even reason to believe that Klinedinst installed a fan so he would not overheat while he was digging…Pennsylvania's secretary of welfare estimated it would have taken 850 trips to move that quantity*

of dirt with a ten-quart pail....An inmate named Bob McKnight, who worked in Eastern State's dental office, stole some plaster so Klinedinst could make a bust to leave in his bed at night while he worked in the tunnel.

Twelve inmates emerged from the one-hundred-foot-long tunnel at seven o'clock in the morning on April 3, 1945. They had reached the surface the previous night but for some reason decided to wait until morning came to break out, which proved to be a mistake. The last person to exit the tunnel was another famous ESP inmate, prolific and charismatic bank robber "Slick" Willie Sutton. Unfortunately for Sutton, he happened to come out of the tunnel right in front of a policeman. All the tunnel escapees were eventually recaptured, one of whom, James Grace, ended up knocking on the front door of the prison eight days later, asking to be let back in. These men were all sent to Klondike, otherwise known as "the Hole," the dark and dingy punishment cells used in the twentieth century. It was later discovered that there were at least thirty partially completed escape tunnels littered throughout the penitentiary grounds.

By the mid-twentieth century, Eastern State Penitentiary was over one hundred years old and was badly showing its age. The buildings needed nearly constant repair. Despite the best efforts of the administration, cells could be freezing cold during the winter and stiflingly hot during the summer, so much so that inmates would sometimes purposefully flood their cells to get some relief from the agonizing heat. Eastern State was declared a National Historic Landmark in 1965, and in September 1969, it was finally decided that the facility would close its doors forever in one year. A former

The remains of the barbershop.

A room in the tuberculosis wing of ESP's hospital in cellblock 3.

guard quoted in Paul Kahan's book said, "A lot of them won't admit it, but they sat down in their cell and cried when this place was going to be shut down. They didn't want to go to Pittsburgh, they didn't want to go to Belfont….They wanted to stay at Eastern."

Twentieth-century inmates called ESP "the House," and when the prison finally saw the last of its inmates leave in January 1970—transferred to other facilities, including the State Correctional Institution at Graterford—it was truly the end of an era. After a riot in Holmesburg prison in northeast Philadelphia, about one hundred of its inmates were placed inside Eastern State Penitentiary temporarily, vacating the building in 1971. After 142 tumultuous years of history, John Haviland's once-revolutionary building stood silent and empty of the living, except for a large population of feral cats. Over the twenty years of its abandonment, nature began to reclaim the property, with some areas of the prison becoming a forest of new trees.

ALTHOUGH THERE ARE SOME vague and unsubstantiated reports handed down of inmates beginning to experience ghosts at Eastern State Penitentiary as early as the 1940s, it was when the prison was finally reopened as a museum and historic site in 1994 that verified stories about encounters with the paranormal began to circulate. Perhaps, after having "the House" to themselves for over twenty years, the many spirits haunting Eastern State Penitentiary decided to make their presence known to those who were disturbing the silence. In all, 1,477 inmates died within the stone walls of

ESP during its 142-year history. Approximately 600 of those deaths were due to tuberculosis, which is why cellblock 3 was eventually turned into a state-of-the-art hospital. Other deaths were caused by murder, suicide, accidents and diseases such as smallpox. So there is no shortage of potential spirits of the dead who may remain trapped within the walls where they breathed their last, hoping for release and freedom that never came.

One of the first people to describe an encounter with the ghosts of Eastern State Penitentiary after its reopening was a locksmith by the name of Gary Johnson, who described his own terrifying experience in a documentary titled *Night Visitors*. Johnson said that as he was working on one of the old, rusty prison cell locks:

> *I had this feeling I was being watched…real intensely. And I turned, and I'm looking down the block, and I know there's nobody there. A couple seconds later I get the same feeling…I'm really being watched…and I turn around, I look down the block, and I don't see anything. And as I started to turn back to the lock, this black shadow just…leaped across the block.… Right here in Philadelphia at Eastern State Penitentiary, you've got a real haunted house.*

This feeling of being watched by a presence you cannot see is the most prevalent feeling by many who work at and visit Eastern State Penitentiary. Former program coordinator Greta Galuszka said in the same documentary, "I would not stay here overnight. The idea of staying in this penitentiary alone is just overwhelming." Senior vice president and director of interpretation Sean Kelley was also interviewed about the paranormal at Eastern State for the 1998 television series *Haunted History*:

> *I'm not a big believer in ghosts, but if there were ghosts anywhere on the planet, you would think they would be here, in a building in which people were forced to spend decades here against their will, many of whom never left the building alive. There's something about this building that has an effect on a lot of people, in that you can just sense there's somebody behind you, in the next room, above you. It can be unnerving, even to a big skeptic like me. Just the other day I was in the front administration building, we were getting ready to do some work up there, and I could swear that on the floor above us, I could hear people murmuring and footsteps. I don't believe it, I don't believe those are ghosts, I think there's got to be another answer. But it was creepy.*

Top: A shower cell in the hospital block.

Bottom: A view of cellblock 14.

The exact identities of the phantoms that roam the decaying walls of the penitentiary are not known, but they continue to make their presence felt. Sounds of footsteps, voices and screams of anguish occasionally echo throughout the cellblocks. The figure of a man in uniform has been seen standing vigil in the guard tower, even though it is now impossible to access. Blocks 4, 6 and 12 are said to be a few of the most active haunted spots, where visitors and staff have suddenly encountered the shadowy silhouettes of former inmates appearing within cells, usually standing eerily still and then suddenly running away down the hallway before vanishing. One of these apparitions was famously caught on camera in a first-season episode of the hit series *Ghost Hunters*, appearing on the upper gallery of cellblock 4. It is one of the few ghostly manifestations that the investigators captured on film that people have not been able to debunk. Two members of the team were so terrified by a ghost suddenly appearing next to them that they ran away screaming.

Every October, Eastern State Penitentiary is filled with tormented screams. For many years, ESP operated a massive haunted house attraction called Terror Behind the Walls as a fundraiser for the historic site, which was rated as one of the best of its kind in the United States. Actors portraying long-dead inmates scared the wits out of thousands of people every year, using many parts of the prison that are not usually open to the public—including the notoriously haunted cellblock 12. Sometimes, actors playing ghostly figures would encounter the real thing. In a 2017 article for the *Metro Philadelphia* newspaper written by Jennifer Logue, Terror Behind the Walls manager Amy Hollaman spoke about two different encounters with the same spirit in cellblock 12 that happened to different actors, years apart:

> *According to many ghost investigators, cellblock 12 is one of the hottest paranormal spots on site. An actor says to me one year, "Amy I can't work on the top floor of cellblock 12 anymore. Can you move my spot?" She asks him why and he replies, "There's a ghost up there. When I was at the edge of the cellblock, it looked like this woman was running towards me screaming and once she got close to me, she turned around and ran back." Hollaman thought his account was "weird" and switched his spot. Three years later, a totally different actor comes to her with a similar story about the second floor of cellblock 12 being haunted: "You'll never believe this, but I think it was a banshee. It was flying down the cellblock towards me screaming. And then turned back."*

I lived across from Eastern State Penitentiary for several years and dreamed of working there as a tour guide. Finally, I got my wish to work at one of the most fascinating historic sites I've ever visited in my life. While on staff at ESP, I had two experiences that unnerved me. One day, I was assigned to sweep cellblock 15, also known as Death Row. No prisoners were ever executed at Eastern State itself, but this is where the most hardened criminals would be housed. I always felt uncomfortable there, like I was being watched. On this particular day, I stepped into the damp cellblock with my broom and suddenly stopped because I heard two men talking. I heard them distinctly; it sounded like they were in the last cell, which was

Cellblock 15: Death Row. It was not fenced off like this when I worked there.

inaccessible. I took a step forward, and I heard one of the voices say, "Shh," and then I heard a man quietly laughing. Suffice to say I did not sweep Death Row that afternoon (although I told my supervisor I did).

The second experience I had was actually on my final day working at Eastern State. At closing time every day, the tour guides each take one cellblock of the prison to sweep out any remaining visitors. You look inside every cell to make sure no one is hiding to try and get an overnight stay. This was in the fall, and it was the first time I had gone through closing a cellblock when it was already dark due to daylight savings time. As I walked down cellblock 4, looking in the cells, I became aware that there was something walking behind me. I heard footsteps, not directly behind me but perhaps ten feet away. As I walked down the cellblock, the footsteps continued. I was terrified, nearly shaking, just trying to keep my eyes focused on the exit at the end of the block. Finally, I made it there and stepped outside, where all the other guides were waiting for me. I finally turned around and looked into cellblock 4. There was no one there. It almost felt as if the ghosts of Eastern State Penitentiary, or one of them anyway, was telling me goodbye—or perhaps trying to get me to stay with them within the walls of this extraordinary national historic landmark, where the past truly feels alive, sometimes in ways that may chill you. As narrator Steve Buscemi says on ESP's audio tour: "If ghosts exist anywhere, they must be here."

CHAPTER 8

A HOST OF HORRORS WITHIN FORT MIFFLIN

If you have ever been on a plane flying to or from the Philadelphia International Airport, you have seen Fort Mifflin. Located very close to the modern airport on Mud Island, Fort Mifflin allows its visitors to take a step backward in time. Dating to 1771, the fort was a pivotal site for the defense of the city during the American Revolution and served as a prison for Confederate soldiers during the Civil War. Although it opened to the public as a historic site in 1962, it is still an active base for the United States Army Corps of Engineers, which makes Fort Mifflin the oldest active military base in the country and the only one built before the Declaration of Independence. Fort Mifflin is one of Philadelphia's most haunted places. The names of its resident ghosts alone are enough to send a chill down your spine; spirits such as the Screaming Lady and the Faceless Man have been witnessed by staff and visitors for decades and continue to make their presence known.

Mud Island was chosen as the site for a protective fort in part due to it being located at the convergence of the Delaware and Schuylkill Rivers. The original structure began to be built in 1771 but was not actually completed until 1776—and not a moment too soon. On September 11, 1777, the Battle of Brandywine was fought. More soldiers fought in this battle than in any other during the American Revolution, with combat lasting for eleven continuous hours. The army of George Washington was defeated by the forces of Sir William Howe, forcing them to retreat and leaving the capital city of Philadelphia open to invasion. But Washington's army was

An overhead view of Fort Mifflin. *Photo by the Historic American Buildings Survey. Public domain.*

not destroyed. He wrote to Congress, "Despite the day's misfortune, I am pleased to announce that most of my men are in good spirits and still have the courage to fight the enemy another day." On September 26, 1777, Sir William Howe's army marched into Philadelphia and began an occupation that would last for nine months. However, the British forces badly needed supplies, and ships were on their way to relieve them. The only thing standing in the way of those British ships was Fort Mifflin.

During the siege beginning on November 10, 1777, 400 soldiers at Fort Mifflin defended it against 250 British ships containing 1,000 enemy troops. Much of the fort was destroyed in the siege, and stone walls still stand today that show evidence of cannon fire. Every night, soldiers at Fort Mifflin repaired the damage as best they could. It is estimated that 1,000 cannonballs were fired at the Fort every hour. Out of the 400 men stationed there, 250 of them were killed during what locals called "the Battle of Mud Island." Finally, on November 15, 1777, the decision was made for the survivors to abandon the fort, as they had run out of supplies and ammunition. They set fire to what remained of Fort Mifflin so that the British would find nothing they could use. They left the fort's flag flying, signaling that although they were leaving, they were not surrendering. When British forces entered Fort Mifflin the following day, they were shocked by the corpses, blood and brain matter littering its ruins. Historians believe that the defense of Fort Mifflin in effect saved the country, due to the fact that it gave Washington's army enough time to retreat and regroup at Valley Forge.

Fort Mifflin remained in ruins until 1793, when rebuilding began. It was at this time that the fort gained its present title; it is named after Thomas Mifflin, who served in the army during the American Revolution and became the first Governor of Pennsylvania. During the Civil War, Fort Mifflin served a different purpose—it became a military prison that held within its dark and dungeon-like casemates Confederate prisoners of war, Union soldiers and civilians. Fort Mifflin's website goes into great detail about the horrific conditions endured by prisoners:

> During the Civil War, Union soldiers could face a variety of punishments for violations of military conduct, including desertion, insubordination, and dereliction of duty. Common punishments included whippings, being branded with a hot iron, and being hung by one's thumbs. Soldiers sentenced to prison time were often forced to perform hard labor with an iron ball and chain attached to their ankle. Union prisoners stayed in one of the large casemates. There were several attempted escapes, including an attempt at a mass uprising in December 1863 and a failed tunnel escape in February 1864....Conditions at Fort Mifflin were poor, as was the case with many military prisons used during the Civil War. The casemates were poorly ventilated and damp. The barracks lacked sufficient windows (many of the window sashes were rotten) or working fireplaces. Foul smells emanated from the moat which was clogged with rotting vegetable matter. Diseases such as typhoid and dysentery affected prisoners and guards stationed at the Fort alike....Prisoners died mostly due to unsanitary conditions, overcrowding, and lack of adequate food and water.

For both World War I and World War II, Fort Mifflin served as an ammunition depot for the United States Navy. The government finally decommissioned the fort in 1954, ending 183 years of service protecting Philadelphia and the nation. It was designated as a National Historic Landmark in 1970 and shortly thereafter opened to the public. Almost

Fort Mifflin. *Photo by Surfsupusa. Wikimedia Commons.*

immediately, people began experiencing strange and frightening things at Fort Mifflin, and unlike many historic sites, the fort has embraced the supernatural side of its history. It's time to meet the ghosts.

VISITORS TO FORT MIFFLIN have sometimes happened upon a reenactor dressed in uniform, busily cleaning his gun. He often looks up at guests as they pass by him and continues with his work. When visitors mention this dedicated reenactor to the staff, they are stunned to be told that there is no reenactor cleaning a gun on site. It is then those visitors realize they have seen a ghost, one that has been affectionately named Amos by Fort Mifflin staff. Who he really was is not known, but since he is seen wearing a uniform from the era of the American Revolution, many have speculated that he is the spirit of one of the many who died in the siege of 1777.

In the blacksmith shop, which is the oldest building at Fort Mifflin, visitors have often heard the sound of the blacksmith at his work. Hoping to experience one of the fort's many living history programs, they are shocked when they enter the blacksmith shop to find nobody there and the building shrouded in eerie silence. It is believed this is the ghost of Jacob Sauer, who was a blacksmith at Fort Mifflin during the time of the Civil War.

The casemates, where prisoners were confined during the Civil War, are said to be the most haunted area of Fort Mifflin. Shadowy figures have often been seen standing or sitting in the cells; they disappear shortly after being seen. Many who venture into these dark and dank rooms have reported a feeling of heaviness or sorrow or a tightness in the chest. Some staff members at Fort Mifflin refuse to enter these areas at all, feeling that they are not alone and that they're being watched by something or someone they cannot see. Near the entrance to the casemates, people have often encountered a man wearing a Union uniform who is sitting and looking down at the ground. As they approach him, the man looks up at them—and he has no face.

The Faceless Man is believed to be the ghost of a private in the Union Army by the name of William H. Howe. Hailing from Perkiomenville, Pennsylvania, William H. Howe joined the Union army to fight for his country. He was a twenty-five-year-old German farmer who quickly gained notoriety on the field of battle for his skill as a marksman. Military records show that fellow soldiers commended him for his "personal courage" as well as his "indomitable will" in the face of the enemy. In December 1862, Howe came down with "inflammation of the bowels," more commonly known as dysentery, one of the most common causes of death for soldiers in the Civil War. Finding the military hospital too full to treat him, William H. Howe left the army and went home to get the medical intervention he needed to save his life. However, the army regarded this as an act of desertion. On June 21, 1863, three officers of the Union army came to William Howe's home to arrest him. Howe fired several shots from inside his home at the officers outside, hoping to scare them away. Unfortunately for Howe, his skill as a marksman worked against him. One of the officers, Abraham Bertolet, was killed by Howe's bullets.

William H. Howe was arrested for desertion and murder and tried by a military court, which sentenced him to death by hanging. He was imprisoned at Fort Mifflin in what is now known as casemate 11, which was rediscovered in 2006. Howe was held in solitary confinement in this small space, and we know he was kept captive there because his signature was found on the walls, still visible today. He was transferred to Eastern State Penitentiary in April 1864 but was returned to Fort Mifflin in August. Even though he was semi-illiterate, William H. Howe wrote two letters to President Abraham Lincoln begging for mercy. His letters were never answered.

On August 26, 1864, William H. Howe ascended the gallows that had been built for his execution. He said to the gathered crowd, "I never sought the life of the man I killed. I never wished it, and I feel God will pardon me for taking it as I did. I know my fellow soldiers and officers in the army never blamed my leaving as I was an invalid and had no hospital to go to in my regiment." After this, a black hood was placed over his head (the reason why many believe his ghost appears as a man without a face), and then his neck was snapped by the noose. William H. Howe was the only prisoner known to be executed at Fort Mifflin, but his ghost remains.

Another terrifying specter haunting Fort Mifflin has been called "the Screaming Lady," who is really the ghost of Elizabeth Pratt. Popular legend suggests that Elizabeth had a daughter who married a man her mother did not approve of. Elizabeth disowned her daughter, who shortly thereafter died of typhoid fever. Unable to bear the loss of her daughter, Elizabeth hanged herself from the balcony of the officer's quarters. As exciting as this story is, it is not the truth. The *History Goes Bump* podcast unearthed the real story of Elizabeth Pratt:

> *The true story of Elizabeth Pratt is much more tragic. She was a real person and the wife of a Seargent Pratt stationed at the fort. However, the family never lived in the Officer's Quarters because those weren't built yet. The family lived in another part of the fort, a spot that does have quite a bit of reported activity. The fort used to have a cemetery (it was moved at some point), and internment records confirm that Elizabeth had two children. One, a son born at the fort, died on July 20, 1802, as an infant. The other is a daughter who died on December 6, 1802—the records include a note that she was a "child," and this indicates that she was twelve years old or younger when she died. Elizabeth herself died on February 11, 1803. All three are thought to have died of yellow fever, annual epidemics of which were common during those years. Yellow fever is spread by mosquitoes, which would be prevalent in the shallow moat and swamps around Fort Mifflin.*

Losing both of her children within such a short period of time understandably plunged Elizabeth Pratt into grief. Ever since she joined them in death, her apparition has been seen in the officer's quarters, and her bloodcurdling screams of anguish echo through Fort Mifflin at night. Former executive director Dori McMunn was interviewed about the ghost of Elizabeth Pratt for an episode of *Haunted History*, saying: "We actually had a tour guide who lived here. He lived just across the street for a while, and he came over more than once in the few years he lived here swearing he heard a woman screaming over here in the fort. Of course, he got in, and there was nobody here." On several occasions, neighbors have called the police in the middle of the night, convinced they hear the screams of a woman being attacked in Fort Mifflin. The police also find the property empty. The lost specter of a young girl has also been seen in the vicinity of the officer's quarters. When visitors ask her what's wrong, she replies she is "looking for Mommy" and then disappears. Some speculate this is the daughter of Elizabeth Pratt who died of yellow fever in 1802, still searching for her mother in the afterlife.

Interviewed for Charles J. Adams III's book *Philadelphia Ghost Stories*, Dori McMunn spoke of another ghost frequently seen by visitors, one they assume is a living person but is not:

> *One day we were having an event on the parade grounds. Everyone was in Revolutionary War uniforms. A woman came up to me praising, absolutely praising a man who led a tour through what we call the "dungeons." I thanked her. She was just gushing about the tour guide. She said he gave her more information than she ever could have imagined. I asked her to tell me what he looked like, so I could commend him. She told me he had a Civil War uniform on. Well, at that, I was taken aback. You see, there was no one on the grounds in a Civil War uniform that day. It was a Revolutionary War reenactment day. But she was positive it was a Civil War uniform, and she said she knew the difference between the two war uniforms.*

As twilight falls at Fort Mifflin, a man is sometimes seen carrying a lantern on the second floor of the soldier's barracks. This is the ghostly lamplighter, still lighting the oil lamps centuries after his death. So, it seems that the host of spirits within Fort Mifflin remain there still, guarding this National Historic Landmark through the gloom of the night. If you visit the fort, I'd be surprised if you didn't experience at least one of its restless souls, bringing its history to life in ways that may make your blood run cold.

CHAPTER 9

THE HAUNTING OF
THE BALEROY MANSION

Chestnut Hill is unquestionably one of the most beautiful neighborhoods in Philadelphia. Filled with affluent homes, picturesque streets and charming local businesses, it is an irresistibly pleasant part of the city to explore. Chestnut Hill is also the location of a thirty-two-room mansion that for decades was called "the most haunted house in America." That house is Baleroy, named after a luxurious French château, and its hauntings were so numerous and unique that Baleroy has been featured in several books and in segments on the paranormal television series *Haunted History* and *Sightings* and has even landed a feature article in *People* magazine.

Part of why Baleroy Mansion became so well known in the vast pantheon of American haunted houses was due to the charm of its owner, Mr. George Gordon Meade Easby. Due to his kindly nature and complete openness, even delight, when discussing the spectral activity inside his ancestral home, Baleroy became justly famous for its plethora of supernatural goings-on. Pretty much every kind of ghostly manifestation you can imagine happened at Baleroy Mansion at one time or another during the tenure of the Easby family's residence in the house. Mr. Easby died in 2005 at the age of eighty-seven, and Baleroy is now owned by others as a private residence. So, please do not go trespassing, as I'm sure the new residents would not hesitate to call the police! But I include Baleroy Mansion in my *Haunted History of Philadelphia* because the past events in the house are so extraordinary and as a tribute to the great man George Meade Easby was.

THE HAUNTED HOUSE IN Chestnut Hill known as Baleroy was built over a century ago in 1911. It was constructed by a carpenter whose name has not be recorded by history. Legend has it that the builder eventually murdered his wife inside the mansion and then committed suicide on the property. A terrible tragedy—but an appropriate beginning for a haunted house that Shirley Jackson would surely be proud of.

In 1926, Baleroy was purchased by the immensely wealthy Easby family, which has a long and illustrious history. They trace their lineage all the way back to Yorkshire, England, in the twelfth century. Easby Abbey, which now lies in ruins and will feature later in the haunting of Baleroy, was named for them. These Easby descendants immigrated from England to America, specifically to the city of Philadelphia, aboard William Penn's ship *Welcome* in 1683. At least seven signers of the Declaration of Independence had Easby blood in their veins.

Most notably, the modern Philadelphia Easbys were descended from General George Gordon Meade, the Union hero of the Battle of Gettysburg who defeated the Confederate army led by General Robert E. Lee during that horrific, bloody and ultimately decisive battle, the turning point of the war. General Meade died of pneumonia in 1872 and is buried in Philadelphia's Laurel Hill Cemetery, the same hallowed city of the dead in which his great-grandson and namesake would be laid to rest 133 years later.

The Easby family that moved into the Baleroy Mansion in 1926 included Major May Stevenson Easby, a veteran of World War I who reinvented himself and made a huge fortune as a banker in Philadelphia; his wife, Henrietta Meade Large Easby, described later by her surviving son as "prim and reserved, a Victorian lady of few words"; and their two children— George Gordon Meade Easby, born in 1918, and May Stevenson Easby Jr., born in 1920. When these children came to live at Baleroy in Chestnut Hill, George was eight years old, and his little brother, called "Steven" or "Stevey," was six.

George Meade Easby said in an interview later in his life:

> *When my brother and I first arrived here at Baleroy, we looked in the fountain. And I saw my reflection in it, but instead of his reflection it was a skeleton. And that really was very unnerving. And shortly after that, he died. Whether that was a warning he was going to…It could have been.*

May Stevenson Easby Jr. died in 1931 of illness when he was just eleven years old. But many, including his surviving older brother, George, believed that after his premature demise, Stevey became one of the many ghosts haunting Baleroy. Shortly after Stevey's funeral, George Meade Easby reportedly saw the apparition of his younger brother in the room where he had died, and over the years, many others would encounter Stevey's spirit looking out of the window of that room. One of them was Dave Beltz, a contractor who did much restoration work at Baleroy in the 1990s. Beltz, interviewed for an episode of *Haunted History*, said:

> *Me being a contractor, working in a lot of other places and then coming here to Baleroy, it seemed really strange. We've had all kind of different encounters. Footsteps, cold drafts, doors opening, ashtrays moving from one side of the table to the other side. We were here working one day doing something and we heard a loud crash.*

Dave Beltz and George Meade Easby investigated the source of this loud crash, and they discovered that a painting had come off the wall and landed ten or fifteen feet away from where it had been hanging. But the nail on which the painting had hung was still tightly in the wall, and the wire on the back of the painting itself was intact and unbroken. The painting was one that depicted Stevey, and it wasn't long after this mysterious incident that Dave Beltz and a coworker saw Stevey's ghost:

> *We were in the courtyard, and I noticed someone looking out the window at me. And I said to my buddy, "Look at that, there's some little guy looking at us." A young kid with blonde hair, I'd say ten at the most, maybe eight. Then it just faded off and my buddy said, "Man, that was really strange." My buddy never came back after that. He was really scared. He just said that he felt somebody stare at him all the time.*

When Dave Beltz informed him of this encounter, George Meade Easby said, "I feel that must have been my brother." What was it like for young George Meade Easby to grow up inside a haunted house? He later said, "Occasionally I would see a figure in the room when it wasn't there. You'd hear people going up the stairs when no one was here. Things like that."

His mother, Henrietta Meade Large Easby, granddaughter of the Civil War general, died in 1962 after a long illness. George Meade Easby said, "I was brought up never to believe in ghosts." However, when his father, Major May Stevenson Easby, died in 1969, he left George a letter to be read after his death, which stated that he had in fact seen ghosts at Baleroy, said that George would see them too and told him not to be afraid. One of the ghosts his father had seen was of his wife and George's mother, Henrietta. George Meade Easby later confided to Charles J. Adams III, the author of *Philadelphia Ghost Stories*, "My mother died before my father, and she came back to him, into his room, and stood by his bed twice. The nurse also saw her. She was wearing a sort of nightgown....Two or three of my friends have seen her." The ghost of Henrietta Easby often appears as a severe-looking woman dressed all in black, walking with a cane. The loud, persistent pounding of a cane on the upper floors where Henrietta Easby died was often heard echoing through the halls of Baleroy in the dead of night.

In 1936, AT THE age of eighteen, George Meade Easby graduated from the Chestnut Hill Academy and then enrolled in classes at the University of the Arts in Philadelphia, studying illustration and painting. His studies were derailed by the United States entering World War II. Easby was drafted into the army, assigned to air patrol. He also began working as a political cartoonist, and one of his works, titled *Air Power Frankenstein*, which showed the United States claiming victory over the Nazi regime of Germany, received a presidential citation from Franklin Delano Roosevelt due to its powerful message of patriotism.

Once the war was over, George Meade Easby began a career as a theater actor and performed in productions at the Cape Cod Playhouse with Gertrude Lawrence, the legendary actress who originated roles in many of Noel Coward's plays, including *Private Lives*, as well as playing the original Anna in the first Broadway production of the musical *The King and I*, which was written especially for her. Easby then went west to Hollywood and found work as an actor and producer for several low-budget films.

However, once his father died in 1969, George Meade Easby returned to Philadelphia, for he was now the sole owner of the Baleroy Mansion. With it, he also inherited more than one hundred thousand antiques collectively worth many millions of dollars, most of which had been handed down within his family over the centuries. Easby set to work on making Baleroy a museum as well as a home. He also was a talk show host on Philadelphia radio for many years and served for twenty-five years as an employee of the U.S. Department of State on its Fine Arts Committee. In 1995, George Meade Easby was appointed as an executive advisor to the under secretary of state. He also loaned many pieces in his priceless collection of antiques to the Department of State, the Philadelphia Museum of Art, the Metropolitan Museum of Art and the White House, all of which were catalogued under the name "the Baleroy Collection."

George Gordon Meade Easby was a great and important man who did much good with his life and his heritage. It is a bonus that he also happened to live in one of America's most haunted houses. He is one of those people that lived a life so incredible you couldn't possibly make it up.

Says psychic Judith Richardson Haines,

> *I'll never forget the first time I walked through the front doors of Baleroy. The first words out of my mouth were, "My God, I can't believe how many spirits are in this house!" When you walk into a place like Baleroy, and you see the silver that was used for the meal by the gentlemen who were ready to sign the Declaration of Independence, you certainly have to pull some wonderful energy from something like that.*

Other than the ghosts of George Meade Easby's little brother, Stevey, and his mother, Henrietta, the remainder of the spirits haunting Baleroy seem to be tied to objects within the house rather than to the house itself. These antiques included a clock that was owned by Marie Antoinette; a pistol, desk, and dining table belonging to ancestor General George Meade; an oil lamp from the ruins of Pompeii; and an eighteenth-century grandfather clock, in front of which the ghost of none other than Thomas Jefferson was reportedly seen standing multiple times.

However, the most famous piece of antique furniture connected with the paranormal activity at Baleroy was a beautiful blue upholstered chair that was once owned by Napoleon Bonaparte, supposedly crafted by a warlock in the eighteenth century, according to some sources. This eventually became known as "the Death Chair," and it was situated in the Blue Room, which George Meade Easby said was the most haunted room in the house. Easby related in an interview, "Well, that's gotten the nickname of the Death Chair because quite a few people who did sit in it died shortly thereafter. So, now I don't let anyone sit in it."

The Death Chair was connected with a Baleroy ghost that Easby called "Amanda." One of the four known people who died after sitting in Napoleon's chair was the former curator of Baleroy, a man named Paul Kimmons. He worked at Baleroy for many years but never experienced anything unusual, pointedly laughing off his employer's tales of Amanda's spirit. One night, Kimmons was giving psychic Judith Richardson Haines a tour of the house when he saw the ghostly figure of a woman in period dress walk down the staircase. "I see that woman! She's there," Paul said.

Several weeks went by, and Judith received a phone call from Paul Kimmons, who was in a state of terror. She later recalled that he said to her,

> *I'm not a hysterical person, but Amanda is following me. I look in my rearview mirror and she's there. I wake up at home and she's there. I'm walking down the street and I catch a glimpse of her out of the corner of my eye. She's scaring me to death. I think I'm losing my mind.*

Finally, Paul Kimmons returned to Baleroy and poured out the whole story to George Meade Easby. An exhausted Paul sat down in Napoleon's blue wingback chair as he spoke. Always in perfect health, Paul Kimmons suddenly died not long after sitting in the chair. After this incident, George Meade Easby placed a silk rope over the arms of the Death Chair and never allowed anyone to sit in it for the rest of his days at Baleroy.

Of the Blue Room itself, George Meade Easby said in an interview:

> *You feel that you're in the presence of...somebody else. Now, many people have gone into that room when it was empty and have told me they feel someone in there. I had some friends here one night shortly after my mother died, and her favorite cabinet was the one behind them. They were sitting in the Blue Room. And it unlocked itself and the doors swung open. And that scared them so, I think they departed.*

A close friend of George Meade Easby named Lloyd Gross was interviewed about the ghosts of Baleroy and the especially eerie events experienced in the Blue Room for episodes of the television series *Haunted History* on the History Channel and *Sightings* on the Sci-Fi Channel in the late 1990s. Lloyd Gross said:

> *I do feel very uncomfortable here. There are many sounds in the night. You hear creaking, and you hear banging and different things. It just seems that there's something very, very strange about it. Not like what any normal house would be.*
>
> *I had been visiting Mr. Easby, and we'd been on the staircase, and it was time for me to go, and I just happened to peek through the glass doors and looked into the Blue Room. And in the arch, it looked like the room was filled with blue smoke or some sort of a cloud. It had no form. It looked like*

it was a blue sort of cloud. And I said to Mr. Easby, "Meade, it looks like it's getting cold out. It looks like dampness in the air or something!" And he said, "Oh no, that's the ectoplasm." I said, "Ectoplasm, what's that?" And he explained it's some sort of energy that's being released or it could be some floating spirits. I don't really know.

I really feel that there is a presence here, and when you're alone here, or it's quiet, it's like no other place. The whole world outside is blocked out, and the inner world here is very, very different.

Lloyd Gross once gave a tour of Baleroy to a local news reporter, and while in the bedroom that had been occupied by George Meade Easby's mother, Henrietta, the tape recorder the reporter had been holding was torn away from his grip and flew across the room. The reporter was so shaken by the experience, Lloyd Gross recalled, that "we had to take him out on the terrace and give him a shot of whiskey." On another occasion, a local minister came to visit the house, and out of nowhere, a copper pot flew through the air and hit him on the head. Although not seriously injured, the minister never set foot within the walls of Baleroy again.

Once psychic Judith Richardson Haines became involved in the hauntings at Baleroy, it seems as if the specter of George Meade Easby's long-dead mother, Henrietta, started communicating with her son from the great beyond. First, he was led to the dusty attic of the house, in the eaves of which he discovered a pair of antique silver candlesticks his mother had hidden there decades earlier that were worth a small fortune. Next, Easby was directed to search a cabinet located in the Blue Room that contained legal documents long forgotten that entitled him to another huge inheritance. On yet another occasion, Judith Richardson Haines was on her way to Baleroy one night when she heard a voice saying the word "Longfellow."

Upon arriving at Baleroy that night, Judith asked George Meade Easby if that meant anything to him, and he replied that his mother Henrietta's favorite poem was "The Children's Hour," written by Longfellow. That evening, when investigating the library at Baleroy, Easby discovered that one old book was sticking out on the shelf. It was a collection of Longfellow's poems that opened directly to the page containing the poem "The Children's Hour," and there was an old envelope, yellowed by time, on which was written in his mother's distinctive handwriting, "To my son, Meade, in the event of my death." The envelope was empty.

On another occasion, George Meade Easby was awakened from a deep sleep by the feeling of someone sitting down on his bed. He looked and saw an impression on the mattress as if a person was sitting there, but there was no one visible. George Meade Easby takes up this tale, related to Charles J. Adams III in his book *Philadelphia Ghost Stories*:

> *It's the kind of thing that happened that when you tell people about it, they think you're making it up. I was in bed, but I don't sleep all night very well. I stay awake a lot, and the time this happened, I'm certain I wasn't dreaming....I saw a monk, dressed in a beige robe, appear in the corner of my room. I had been thinking of a little business deal—should I do it, or shouldn't I? Then the monk spoke: "NO, Mr. Easby. NO!" Then the monk dissolved...so I didn't.*

The next morning, George Meade Easby woke to find that his right arm was bruised black and blue, as if someone had grabbed him during the night with unnatural strength. He decided not to go through with the business deal and later discovered that if he had, he would have lost a huge amount of money. Later, on a trip to the ancestral Easby Abbey in Yorkshire, England, George learned for the first time that at Easby Abbey, the monks always wore beige robes.

There is also an unusual haunting that occurs outside of Baleroy's walls—a phantom car. This eerie visitation usually happens in the late evening, although it has occasionally occurred during the day. Interviewed for *Philadelphia Ghost Stories*, George Meade Easby said, "We don't see it, but very often we'll hear a car go by in the driveway. It goes right by the window. Many people have heard it, and we look, but there's no car there. My theory is that it's someone in my family coming back to check and see if I'm behaving!"

> *Living here is really an adventure, I feel, and you're never quite sure what is going to happen.*
>
> *—George Gordon Meade Easby*

After a lifetime filled with joy and extraordinary experiences of all kinds, George Meade Easby died on December 11, 2005, at Keystone Hospice in Wyndmoor, Pennsylvania, at the age of eighty-seven years. He had been suffering from "dementia of the Alzheimer type" for several years prior to his death. Easby was survived by his partner of twelve years, Robert Yrigoyen, to whom he left Baleroy and all its contents. A lawsuit was brought to challenge the will of George Meade Easby by the Commonwealth of

The grave of George Gordon Meade Easby at Laurel Hill Cemetery. *Photo by Dwkaminski. Wikimedia Commons.*

Pennsylvania and a local hospital which had also been left money in Easby's will, claiming that Robert Yrigoyen had practiced "undue influence" and that Easby was not of sound mind when he prepared the will leaving the bulk of his estate to Robert.

Robert Yrigoyen stated in the court record that he "was the decedent's longtime friend, lover, and Life Partner, and had lived with the decedent in the functional equivalent of a marital relationship for over ten years prior to the decedent's death." Quoting directly from the court records, which are public:

> *As the testimony evolved, George Meade Easby emerged as a "private," "complex," and "very closeted" person who behaved differently depending on whether he was in gay or heterosexual company. Like the film Rashomon, the image of Meade that emerged varied significantly depending on the perspective of the narrator or witness....Friends who knew Meade well testified to his strong, tender feelings for Robert. Lady Wedgewood recalled Meade describing Robert as his "dear, dear friend, how wonderful his life was because Robert was in it, and that basically he couldn't live without Robert." Perhaps the most vivid description of the relationship of Meade and Robert was presented by their younger friend, Walter Opdyke, who recalled that when he made some "off-hand" remark about Robert, Meade chastised him and said, "Don't say that. I love him." Opdyke then recalled that "Meade said that he would like to go, I think it was to Vermont, it was whatever state at the time had just passed a law validating gay marriages and that he would like to go there and marry Robert."—The record establishes that Robert and Meade had a longstanding, loving relationship, at the end of which Robert not only gently cared for Meade by making sure he had 24-hour nursing care, but also by assuring him the opportunity to meet with his friends in his beloved Baleroy. Based on the record presented, the respondent established by clear and convincing evidence the absence of undue influence.*

This, I feel, is a landmark court decision, years before same-sex marriage was legally recognized by the Commonwealth of Pennsylvania. Robert Yrigoyen received his inheritance as his husband, in all but legal name, wished him to. George Gordon Meade Easby now rests in his grave at Laurel Hill Cemetery, the same city of the dead where his ancestor, General George Meade, has been since his own death in 1872.

The antiques and furniture of Baleroy was sold at auction to museums and collectors all over the world. I wonder where the Death Chair is now, and if it has claimed any further victims. In 2012, Robert Yrigoyen sold the Baleroy Mansion itself to new owners, who maintain it to this day as a private residence. The current owners have experienced unexplained noises in the house, as well as seeing the ghost of Stevey, the little brother of George Meade Easby, who died there so long ago. They have also heard the phantom car coming up the driveway when no car is to be seen and been unnerved by lights in the house turning on and off by no human hand.

In an article published by the *Chestnut Hill Local* newspaper on October 25, 1984, just in time for Halloween, George Gordon Meade Easby said:

> *When I leave here, I'm coming back to haunt them. If they don't take good care of this place I'm going to be right back here after them.*

In a 2015 newspaper article written by Kevin Feeley, the current owners of the Baleroy Mansion did say, "We're Catholic. And just for good measure, you have the house blessed when you move in…even if it's not a haunted house…but we did tell the priest to take his time."

CHAPTER 10

CASTLE GHOSTS AT ARCADIA UNIVERSITY

Just north of Philadelphia in the town of Glenside, Pennsylvania, you will find Arcadia University. It was originally established nearly 170 years ago in Beaver, Pennsylvania, as the Beaver Female Seminary in 1853. Just nineteen years later, in 1872, it became Beaver College. In 1925, it moved its campus to Jenkintown, Pennsylvania, and moved for the final time in 1928 after purchasing the lavish Harrison estate in Glenside, including the magnificently gothic Grey Towers Castle, which became a National Historic Landmark in 1985. As the twenty-first century approached, it was decided that the college needed to change its name due to it being filtered out of internet searches. The institution applied for and received university status and, in 2001, was reborn as Arcadia University. Like many places of higher learning throughout the United States and abroad, Arcadia has its fair share of macabre and ghostly legends that are passed down from student to student through the generations.

Full disclosure: I attended Arcadia University as an undergraduate from 2003 to 2007, earning a bachelor of fine arts in acting. The tales of the campus being haunted were widely known and talked about, especially those involving Grey Towers Castle. A student group known as the Society for Castle Restoration conducted ghost tours of the castle and the campus each year during the month of October, furthering the belief in the spooky side of academic life at Arcadia. The second and third floors of the castle, which were originally used as bedrooms for the family and servants who lived there, are now student housing, and rooms there are highly sought after by students

Grey Towers Castle. *Photo by Peetlesnumber1. Wikimedia Commons.*

who want a chance to live in Hogwarts. I mean this literally. The architect of Grey Towers, Horace Trumbauer, based his design for it on Alnwick Castle in England, the exteriors of which were used as Hogwarts for the Harry Potter movies. Sadly, I never got the chance to live in a haunted castle. I am most certainly not still bitter about it years later!

More than any other site featured in this book, I would file the ghost stories about the campus under the category of urban legends. Although we know a bit about the family who built Grey Towers Castle, there is little in the way of behind-the-scenes details in existing historical records. Rest assured, Arcadia University is haunted, and over the years, stories have been passed down to explain the paranormal occurrences experienced by faculty and students, including myself. Whether these origin stories for the campus's hauntings stem from truth or are products of imaginative storytelling and embellishment over the decades is impossible to know for sure, but as folklore that is still thriving more than ever at Arcadia, I believe they deserve to be included in this book. I will begin first with what is known to be historically factual and then dive into the legends. They are good and grisly, I assure you, perfect for a dark and stormy night.

William Welsh Harrison was born on Pine Street in Philadelphia in 1850, only three years before the founding of what would later become Beaver College and then Arcadia University. His education began at the Germantown Academy and culminated in his graduation from the prestigious University of Pennsylvania in 1869. As soon as William finished school, he followed in his father's footsteps, working at the Franklin Sugar Refinery in Philadelphia as a "sugar manufacturer" and manager, both jobs at which he excelled. During this period of history, the Franklin Sugar Refinery was not only one of the largest sugar factories in the United States, but it was also one of the largest in the entire world. It is estimated that 90 percent of the sugar refined in North America came from this single factory, making William Welsh Harrison an extremely rich man. A 2013 article in the *Philadelphia Inquirer* written by Rick Nichols provides a glimpse of the extreme lengths taken to keep secret the Franklin Sugar Refinery's methods as well as protect the huge profits it generated for its owners:

> *In order to mystify New York refiners eager to learn its trade secrets, it was equipped with a Willy Wonka-like room crammed with pipes and valves that was entirely a sham; the valves would regularly be opened and closed to no actual purpose, their job simply to throw industrial spies off the scent.*

William Welsh Harrison married Bertha Whyte, and they had two children together. Their first child was a daughter named Geraldine, born in 1881. Just three years later, in 1884, Bertha Whyte Harrison gave birth to a son, William Welsh Harrison, Jr. Tragically, their eldest daughter, Geraldine, died in a horse-riding accident in 1903. She was only twenty-two years old at the time of her death and was survived by her husband, John Childe Anderson. Their son, William Jr., outlived both his parents and died in 1965. All are buried in Laurel Hill Cemetery.

In 1881, William Welsh Harrison purchased what was known as the Rosedale Hall estate in the town of Glenside. The estate, at this time, comprised some 138 acres of land. In 1891, Harrison decided to enlarge Rosedale Hall itself as well as add a gatehouse and improve the stables on the property. To do this, he hired Horace Trumbauer, a twenty-three-year-old architect with a bright future ahead of him. In 1892, William Welsh Harrison sold the Franklin Sugar Refinery for an enormous sum, making him even richer than before, with a net worth of $3 million, which would be almost $92 million in today's money. In hindsight, this increase in wealth was fortuitous, because on January 14, 1893, at around one o'clock in the morning, Rosedale Hall caught fire and burned to the ground. It was a snowy winter's night, and the Harrison family and their servants all managed to escape the blaze and seek shelter in the stables.

Harrison again engaged architect Horace Trumbauer, this time to rebuild the family home on an even grander scale, and what rose from the ashes of the fire became Grey Towers Castle. It was finished in 1898 and consisted of forty rooms with lushly decorated interiors that were inspired by and rivaled the greatest castles of Europe. Mark Meredith describes Grey Towers in loving detail on the website www.househistree.com:

> *Grey Towers Castle measures a massive 225-feet across with a depth of 185-feet. Built with gray stone quarried from nearby Chestnut Hill it is trimmed with Indiana limestone. Its six towers of varying sizes are finished with Gothic-style battlements and the facades are interspersed with gargoyles, other traditional Gothic architectural features, and a carved copy of the Harrison coat-of-arms. Said to have been built without a single nail, construction costs ran to $250,000. After it was finished, it was considered to be the third largest house in the country and seeing it complete Harrison wrote, "The name Grey Towers seemed more appropriate than Rosedale Hall."…The principal room coming off the Great Hall on the left (on what is the south side of the castle) is the walnut-paneled Dining Room which features columns and caryatids reminiscent of those at the Château de Fontainebleau. At the other end of the room, glass doors once opened up into a since demolished circular conservatory and leading off to the west was the Breakfast Room and beyond that kitchens etc. On the other side of the Hall directly opposite the Dining Room is the Drawing Room, better known as the Rose Room and decorated in the style of Louis XV. A pair of sliding doors in the center of the room open onto the Ballroom, also known as the Mirror Room. The Mirror Room was ordered in France and shipped to America along with the craftsmen needed to assemble it. Its Renaissance-inspired ceiling is painted showing the four seasons as women.…The bedroom suites were on the second floor with their own dressing rooms, boudoirs, fireplaces and marble baths. Despite the air of antiquity prevalent throughout the house, it was fitted with electricity and every modern convenience.*

The final years of William Welsh Harrison's life were troubled. Harrison discovered that one of his best friends, Francis Ralston Welsh, who had also acted as his broker, had stolen $239,000 from him over the period of a decade. Harrison sued him and appeared in court, but the stress of this personal betrayal weighed heavily on his mind and body. William Welsh Harrison had a heart attack in Grey Towers Castle and died there on March 4, 1927, at the age of seventy-six. His widow, Bertha Whyte Harrison, sold the estate to Beaver College two years later in 1929 for the sum of $712,500. She herself died in 1933 at the age of seventy-five, and both are buried in the family mausoleum at Laurel Hill Cemetery.

In 1962, Beaver College moved the entirety of its operations to the Grey Towers estate. Mark Meredith writes,

> *Today, the ground floor of the castle is home to several of the university's administrative offices and conference/events rooms. The upper two floors have been sympathetically converted into suite-style dormitories for select freshmen, giving them an opportunity to experience life here as the Harrisons had done—with perhaps an added ghost or two.*

That concludes the history of Grey Towers Castle, and now we'll move on to the ghostly urban legends of the estate that is now home to Arcadia University, of which there are many. Understandably, most of the hauntings on campus are associated with the castle itself. According to stories that have been handed down through generations of students, faculty and staff, the marriage between William and Bertha Harrison was not a happy one. By the time Grey Towers was finished in 1898, the couple's union had deteriorated so completely that they each lived in separate wings of the castle—William lived in one, and Bertha and the two children occupied the other. The student housing today reflects this, with male students occupying one wing and women the other. Perhaps this explains why the ghosts of the Harrisons remain.

Allegedly, William Welsh Harrison conducted many affairs with the maids who worked in the castle, and many secret passages and tunnels were constructed to make it easy for Harrison to quietly sneak his mistresses into his bedroom. Bertha Harrison knew of her husband's many infidelities but refused to divorce for the sake of their children and to maintain the family's status in high society. However, one day, Bertha could take the humiliation of her husband's affairs no longer. She waited in a small room on the second floor of the castle until one of the maids entered the room. Mrs. Harrison locked the door, and it was then that the maid saw the butcher knife in her hand. The maid screamed and tried to escape the room, but Mrs. Harrison stabbed her to death in a jealous rage, the blood from the maid's many wounds staining the white walls crimson. Since the Harrisons were extremely wealthy, this brutal murder of a servant was covered up and the maid's body buried in an unmarked grave somewhere on the grounds of the estate.

After the maid's corpse was disposed of, the white walls of the room where her murder had taken place naturally had to be repainted to cover up the blood. However, a few days after the room had been painted, the bloodstains came back. The room was repainted again. Still, the telltale bloodstains reappeared after a few days. Finally, the walls of the room on the second floor were painted a deep red to hide the blood. In Arcadian legend, it became known as the Red Room, and its door was kept locked for many years. An alumnus named Christopher Klimovitz spoke about the haunting of the Red Room for the *History Goes Bump* podcast in 2017:

> *Rumor has it that some years ago, there was a séance done there, an amateur séance with a Ouija board. Apparently, some students decided to get together and wanted to summon the spirits. Well, you know how people say, "Don't mess with the spirits; things will happen," and it did. Apparently, someone was attacked, apparently it frightened them terribly, apparently someone was sent to the hospital, and the rumor is that when you get there, Ouija boards are banned from campus…and that has been taken down in the mythology of the school.*

In a 2016 blog post on the university's website entitled "Is Arcadia Haunted," author Spencer Potts also brought up the legend that Ouija boards are banned from the castle. Nick Kirkstadt, a staff member at Arcadia, responded: "Ouija boards are not banned from campus, and they will not be confiscated. I believe the rumor stems from an incident a few years back, but there is no reason that students cannot own or use a Ouija board here at Arcadia." What is interesting about this statement is that it does suggest that the tale of a séance gone wrong in the Red Room has some basis in truth. There was "an incident," but exactly what happened, we do not know.

It was actually during my four years as a student at Arcadia University that the infamous Red Room was finally unlocked and turned into one of the offices for the financial aid department, in which I worked. I remember my excitement at getting a chance to peek into the legendary Red Room, and its walls were still painted crimson. One of my supervisors worked in that office, and she always said that she felt uncomfortable there, constantly looking over her shoulder while sitting at her desk, as if she was being watched.

According to some students who have lived in the castle, the sounds of muffled screams can sometimes be heard echoing in the locked Red Room in the dead of night.

The ballroom, or Mirror Room, on the first floor of the castle contains another ghostly legend, one that isn't nearly as gruesome. It is said that often during special events and dances that are held in the Mirror Room, people have seen the phantom figures of William and Bertha Harrison dancing in the panes of glass. The story goes that if you are dancing with your beloved in the Mirror Room and you see the Harrisons, you will marry the person you are dancing with. Now, this contradicts the tales about William and Bertha's supposedly dysfunctional marriage, but it's a good story all the same, isn't it?

The Grand Staircase also has a restless spirit, that of a little girl. According to legend, she was a friend and playmate of the Harrison's daughter, Geraldine. On a winter's day, the little girl was running down the staircase at lightning speed, eager to get out into the snowy wonderland that awaited her outside of the castle. Unfortunately, the long scarf she was wearing around her neck got caught on the banister, yanking the little girl's body backward and throwing her over, breaking her neck. Her body was found hanging from the banister by her scarf, and her ghost has been seen by generations of students ever since. Charles J. Adams III interviewed a graduate student who wished to remain anonymous for his 2000 book *Montgomery County Ghost Stories*, and she recounted her experience:

> *I was down at the desk by the main entrance when I was distracted and saw something on the staircase. It was smoky, gray, filmy—that's the best way I can describe it. It was weird. It was small, like a little child would be, and it seemed to sway slowly, as if it was hanging over the side of the railing. Now is the really weird part. I mentioned something about it to a friend a couple hours later. She got very serious and told me I must have seen the ghost of the little girl. That's when I told her, and I'm telling you now, that up to that point I had never heard any story about any little girl's ghost in the castle. I guess I was just out of the loop, but I had no idea.... All I know is that I never before and never since have seen anything like it. If it was a ghost, so be it. It didn't bother me. But I do really feel for the little girl if her spirit remains there. Then again, if you have to haunt some place, it might as well be place as beautiful as that.*

In addition, students who run quickly down the grand staircase, perhaps running late for class, have reported that they feel something pulling them back, as if encouraging them to slow down so they don't experience the little girl's tragic fate. The excited laughter of a small child has been heard echoing through the great hall, and the piano in the music room sometimes plays by itself when there is no one physically present in the room, the notes discordant and amateurish, as if a young kid was doing it.

The former bedrooms of the Harrison family and their servants on the second and third floors are now student housing, and they are also subject to paranormal activity. Students have heard footsteps walking the halls only to look out their doors and see that no one is there. The unsettling noise of a cane pounding on the floor has also been heard, and legend has it this is the ghost of William Welsh Harrison, who used to pound on his bedroom floor as a signal for his servants to bring him more to drink. A rocking chair in the upper floors has also been seen and heard to rock by itself, supposedly occupied by the melancholy spirit of Bertha Harrison, mourning the death of her daughter, Geraldine. In the castle dorm rooms, students have also heard the eerie sounds of kids singing nursery rhymes in rooms that were originally occupied by the Harrison's children. They have seen faces appear in mirrors, as well as closet doors opening by themselves and lights turning on and off without explanation.

Another haunted area of the castle is its basement, which contains the entrances to the over five hundred feet of dark and cobweb-adorned tunnels that run underneath the grounds of the campus. The tunnels have always been off-limits, and many of them have been blocked off for safety reasons, but there are several that still exist. A 2009 *Philadelphia Inquirer* article written by Susan Snyder tells the story of a public safety officer named Roy Surma, who was patrolling the basement of the castle at two thirty in the morning. He said, "Just as I adjusted my radio, something clamped on my wrist. Of course, there was nothing around me. What it was, I have no idea." In the same article, maintenance supervisor John Hagerty reported, "When you're in the basement, you'll see things out of the corner of your eye, and you'll swear somebody just walked by."

One final specter haunting Grey Towers Castle is known as Abigail. The stories passed down through the years say that Abigail was a young woman from a wealthy family who often stayed with the Harrisons on their grand estate. She reportedly fell in love with a servant named Toby who worked in the stables and planned to elope with him. However, Abigail's parents discovered this upstairs/downstairs romance and locked Abigail in her bedroom on the second floor of the castle. The following morning, the Harrisons and their guests were enjoying breakfast on the terrace

The stables of the Grey Towers estate, now known as Murphy Hall. *Photo by Acronach. Wikimedia Commons.*

and remarked that Abigail was not present. At that same moment, they noticed that there was red fluid slowly dripping down the glass walls of the atrium. They looked up at the glass roof and were horrified to see the bloody corpse of Abigail. Sometime during the night, Abigail had jumped from her bedroom window and impaled herself on the iron spikes of the atrium. Ever since then, people have seen the ghostly figure of a woman in clothing from another time wandering through the woods at the edge of campus. Many believe it is the heartbroken spirit of Abigail, still trying to find Toby in the afterlife.

Grey Towers Castle is not the only haunted location at Arcadia University. The stables, now known as Murphy Hall, are haunted by the phantom of a young boy who, it is said, was accidentally trampled to death by horses. Within Murphy Hall's corridors, students and faculty have often seen a young boy who looks to be about ten years old. When they ask him what he is doing there, he disappears. Spruance Hall was originally a maintenance building on the Harrison estate, also the home of the chief engineer employed by the family. It is said that this engineer was also tragically killed here when one of the boilers overheated and exploded. Spruance Hall now houses Arcadia University's theater, where I spent most of my four years as an undergraduate. It was not uncommon to see the shadowy, almost

Spruance Hall, now home to Arcadia University's theater and fine arts programs. *Photo by Acronach. Wikimedia Commons.*

transparent figure of a man walk across the stage when locking up the theater for the night. I recall vividly that during one class I had in the theater, we kept hearing loud banging noises and footsteps echoing on the lighting grids above the stage. Finally, the professor got up on stage, looked up and said they saw nobody up there. The professor shouted upward, "I don't like that!" The mysterious sounds stopped.

In Dilworth Hall, one of several dormitories on campus, people have seen a male student run down the length of the third-floor hallway between two and three o'clock in the morning and jump out of a window, only to vanish. Arcadia lore suggests this may be the ghost of a long-ago student who took his own life and is doomed to repeat his final moments. According to legend, another dorm called Heinz Hall was built over the site of an old cemetery. Approximately 250 bodies were removed before the dorm was built— except one corpse was forgotten. This is the ghost that has become known as Max. Students who live in Heinz Hall report odd happenings, such as showers turning on by themselves, lights being turned off by unseen hands and various other unexplained phenomena. As a proud alumnus, I highly recommend checking out Arcadia University if you're in search of higher learning. You'll receive a great education, and it's very likely you'll meet at least one of the campus ghosts during your time on the grand old estate.

CHAPTER 11
POLTERGEISTS AND MURDER AT THE INN

Located in Merion Station, Pennsylvania, just eight miles from Philadelphia, stands a historic structure known for over two hundred years as the General Wayne Inn. A tavern first opened on the site in 1704, standing on land that had been acquired by William Penn. Originally known as the Wayside Inn, over the decades, it changed ownership and name several times, becoming the Tunis Ordinary and then Streeper's Tavern. Located on a busy road heading toward Lancaster and the west, it was an enormously popular resting place and watering hole and even served as a post office presided over by Ben Franklin himself for a time.

During the American Revolution, the building became even busier as several major battles were fought nearby. On September 13, 1777, General Anthony Wayne stayed at the tavern overnight while his troops slept in the field outside. Wayne earned the nickname "Mad Anthony" due to his relentlessness in battle, which often led to decisive victories but sometimes to foolish defeats. The next night, September 14, 1777, George Washington and the Marquis de Lafayette also stayed there and enjoyed a hearty breakfast before continuing on to war. Because of its ideal location on a main road, the inn was frequented by both patriots and Hessian soldiers, who were German mercenaries fighting on the side of the British.

In 1795, General "Mad" Anthony Wayne returned to the tavern, and it was after this visit that the building was named after him. It became known as the General Wayne Inn, which until the early twenty-first century advertised itself as the oldest continuously operating inn in North America. It was added to the National Register of Historic Places in 1976. The General Wayne Inn is known not only for its history but also for its hauntings. The inn has been featured in numerous books, as well as in a segment for the television series *Unsolved Mysteries*, and finally, it was the subject of an episode of *Forensic Files*, for reasons I will explain in due time.

An eighteenth-century print of General Anthony Wayne.

Before I tell you about the ghosts of the General Wayne Inn, and the tragedy that marked its recent history, I feel I must pay a small, macabre tribute to the namesake of the inn, General Anthony Wayne. He died just one year after his triumphant return to the inn, on December 15, 1796. The official cause of death was a stomach ulcer, but some historians have raised the possibility that Wayne may have been poisoned by his second-in-command, General James Wilkinson, who assumed full command after General Wayne died. The truth can never be known, but Mad Anthony Wayne was laid to rest in a grave at Fort Presque Isle, located in Erie, Pennsylvania.

Thirteen years later, in 1809, General Anthony Wayne's son Isaac ventured to Erie to claim his father's remains and take them back to the family burial plot located in Radnor, Pennsylvania. However, when General Wayne's body was exhumed, it was perfectly preserved, as if he had just been buried yesterday. Isaac Wayne had brought only a small cart with him to transport his father's remains. So a local doctor cut the corpse of General Anthony Wayne into conveniently sized pieces and boiled them in a huge kettle, removing the flesh from the bones. The bones of General Wayne went home with his son Isaac and were buried in the family plot. The flesh, kettle and the water used to boil the dissected corpse were reburied in the original grave. Thus, General Anthony Wayne is one of few in history to have two legitimate burial sites. Legend says that on January 1, his birthday, the ghost of Mad Anthony Wayne can be seen walking the road between his first and second graves, trying to reunite his flesh and bones.

Adding to the creepy historical atmosphere of the General Wayne Inn, another one of its frequent guests was Edgar Allan Poe, who is said to have revised a portion of his immortal poem "The Raven" while sitting at a table by the fireplace. Poe even used a friend's diamond ring to scratch his initials—E.A.P—into one of the glass windows at the General Wayne Inn. Sadly, the piece of window glass bearing Poe's initials was accidentally destroyed in the 1970s due to construction work. But some say that his spirit has been seen at the inn, sitting at a lonely table.

When the long-running television show *Unsolved Mysteries* decided to feature the ghosts of the General Wayne Inn for its Halloween episode in 1988, the producers reached out to renowned parapsychologist Dr. Michaeleen C. Maher to assist with the interviews and provide scientific analysis. She later published an academic paper on the experience, "Quantitative Analysis of the General Wayne Inn," which is the source for most of the quotes that follow in this chapter. Maher writes:

> *For more than 50 years, the inn served as a polling site for the Lower Merion Township, and the first reported sighting of a ghost dates back to the election of 1848. A woman who had gone to the cellar to retrieve a box of fresh ballots reported to her supervisor when she returned that she had encountered a soldier in a green coat down there. (Hessians wore green uniforms with yellow lapels.) The basement sighting of the soldier was included in the supervisor's official report to the Board of Elections. Legend has it that…a secret tunnel had been built by the revolutionaries that led from the inn's cellar to an unobtrusive part of the neighboring field. Although accounts differ, one version holds that when a young Hessian soldier was sent to the cellar to procure wine…he was ambushed and killed by revolutionaries hiding there. They promptly buried his body in the tunnel so that it would not give them away. Locals residing in what is now Lower Merion Township believe that the ghost of the Hessian soldier still haunts the inn.*

Alice Gormley, a hostess who first started working at the General Wayne Inn in 1960, also went on the record for *Unsolved Mysteries* about seeing the ghost of the Hessian soldier. She said,

> *I was walking through the dining room, and I heard someone call my name…so I walked out of* [the dining room] *to see if it was the manager, and I saw this apparition, this person, on the stairs. He had this uniform on…a Revolutionary War soldier.…He looked so startled, and when I said, "Can I help you?" he just disappeared. The bartender looked at me and said, "What's the matter? You look like you saw a ghost." And I said, "Well, I think I did."*

For her book *In Search of Ghosts: Haunted Places in the Delaware Valley*, Elizabeth P. Hoffman interviewed the General Wayne Inn's longtime owner, Barton Johnson. He said there was another employee who had witnessed the ghost of the Hessian soldier. One Saturday morning, Bart Johnson arrived at the inn to discover that the main dining room was in a state of disarray. Half of the room had been cleaned, the other half had not and the man employed to clean the building was nowhere to be found. Worried, Johnson called the employee, who was at home, and told him to come back and finish his work. There was a long pause, and then the employee said:

> *I'm not coming back today. No sir, no way. When I was about half done in the dining room, a noise made me look up. There in the far corner was standing a big soldier in one of those old-fashioned uniforms. He was just looking at me. So, I put down my broom, put on my coat, and walked out. I'm not coming back today.*

Perhaps the most unusual and disturbing encounter related to the Hessian soldier's ghost happened to a maître d' who had worked at the General Wayne Inn for many years. Dave Rogers related his chilling encounter on *Unsolved Mysteries*:

> *I was maître d' at the time, and we were closing the restaurant up for the night. I was in the kitchen, and I was starting to go out, and I looked up. I only saw it for a split second….It was just a head, sitting on this chest of drawers. It didn't register with me right away, but when I got out to the bar area, it was like I hit a brick wall. I stopped dead in my tracks and started saying, "I saw a head! I saw something! I saw a head!" I only saw it for a second, but I…I'll never forget it. It…had a very painful expression…thin, black, slicked-back hair. His ears stuck out a little bit. He had pencil-thin eyebrows and a pencil-thin mustache. And no neck or anything, just—just a head. That's all I saw….He was just sitting there, looking at me. The other employees that were there with me in the bar area, they all said, "Uh oh, he saw something, let's get out of here." And we all packed up and we left.*

There was also a bartender at the inn who saw the ghost of the soldier in the basement. After that, the bartender refused to ever go down into the basement again. He would have waiters go down and bring up the extra liquor when he was working. Finally, Bart Johnson decided to hold a séance at the inn to try and communicate with the spirit of the Hessian soldier. New Jersey psychics Jean and Bill Quinn led the séance, which took place in the dining room where George Washington slept in 1777. Just as the séance began, the heavy front doors of the dining room, which were locked, opened by themselves. To owner Bart Johnson's surprise, Jean and Bill Quinn said that the General Wayne Inn was haunted by not just one but seventeen different ghosts. They also provided the spirit of the Hessian soldier with a name—Wilhelm.

Another psychic, Mike Benio, was staying a few nights at the General Wayne Inn, and each night he was visited by Wilhelm's apparition, standing at the foot of his bed. Benio eventually told Bart Johnson of these spectral appearances, saying that Wilhelm's ghost had told him that he had been murdered and his bones were hidden in the basement. Since Mike Benio's primary job was as a building contractor, Bart Johnson gave him permission to start carefully excavating the portion of the basement where the ghost had said his body was buried. Surprisingly, Benio soon unearthed a small room in the basement that no one knew existed. It was not shown on any floorplans of the inn. Inside of this secret room, human bones were found. They were removed and given a proper burial, and the hidden room was bricked up once again.

This seems to have calmed down the appearances of Wilhelm's ghost, but there was far more paranormal activity at the General Wayne Inn that remained unexplained. Much of this can be described as poltergeist activity, spirits physically moving objects or being mischievous to get the attention of the living. Glasses and bottles in the bar would shake all at the same time for no discernable reason. A chandelier would swing back and forth by itself when no breeze or draft was present. Cars in the parking lot would have their lights and horns turn on when no one was in the vehicle. Towels in the kitchen and furniture in the dining rooms would move on their own.

The bar was especially active. Dave Rogers recalled:

> I heard footsteps, just as if somebody was walking the entire length of the bar, all the way down. And the people sitting in the bar stools felt the floorboards moving. And I was facing the direction that…the footsteps were going down. And I did not see anybody. All I heard were the footsteps. I heard them loud and clear. And they went the entire length of the bar and when they got to the end of the bar they stopped. And the customers were looking at each other like, "What was that?"

Former owner Bart Johnson recalled other phenomena in the bar area that were more amusing than frightening. Interviewed for *Unsolved Mysteries*, he said:

> *I enjoy these ghosts. They don't bother me at all. I think they come up with some real clever little things. When we get busy at the bar…the girls would end up on all the bar stools…and that would be thirteen, fourteen, fifteen girls sitting there….And because of the lack of additional seating, the guys all stand behind their wife, girlfriend, whatever. And at ten, eleven o'clock at night, one of our entities will blow on the back of a girl's neck. And the girl will turn around and say to her boyfriend, "What did you do that for?" And the next minute, the next girl would feel breath on the back of her neck….All the way down the bar. And the poor guys, they really were doing nothing except listening to the music and maybe drinking their beer or whatever they were drinking. And it was very interesting. And the first time I saw it, I couldn't believe it. It would take him a half an hour to go from one end of the bar to the other end….And I would purposefully position myself so I could see if it was going to happen again—the blowing on the back of the girls' necks….I knew when the first one started, it would continue all the way down to the end of the bar. It always did.*

Another strange incident occurred when a local news station aired a segment about the haunting of the General Wayne Inn for Halloween. Staff and customers filled the bar to watch the television coverage. As soon as footage of the inn began to play on the news broadcast, the image on the TV began to slowly turn clockwise. It continued to do so until the segment on the hauntings finished and then returned to normal. No one else in the area who watched the news that night observed the television image turning, only those at the General Wayne Inn.

In 1995, Bart Johnson, after twenty-five years of ownership, sold the General Wayne Inn to an executive chef named Jim Webb and his business partner, Guy Sileo. Both men were excited to bring this national historic site back into prominence for a new generation of patrons. They had been well informed about the inn's long-standing reputation for being haunted but, by all accounts, accepted the supernatural aspect of the building's history. However, Jim Webb's wife, Ruby, was not shy about describing the fear she felt in the place. Ruby Webb later said in an interview: "I was afraid to be by myself in one area of the restaurant. I would consider it creepy…maybe even somewhat evil."

On December 27, 1996, employees found Jim Webb dead on the floor of his third-floor office at the General Wayne Inn. One of the employees first thought he had fallen and hit his head, due to the large knot that was visible on his forehead. Police and medical examiners later discovered that Jim Webb had been shot in the back of the head, and the knot was actually the .25-caliber bullet that had failed to exit the skin on his temple. Police kept the manner of death to themselves, refusing to tell even his wife and family the cause of Jim's death. They did this hoping that the killer would reveal information about the murder that could only be known by the police and by the perpetrator. Evidence showed that Jim Webb had been killed the night before his body was discovered, on December 26, 1996—the day after Christmas. Jim Webb was survived by his wife, Ruby, and two young children. He was only thirty-one years old.

Because Jim Webb was murdered in a third-floor office that was difficult to access, it seemed immediately clear to investigators that the culprit had to have known the layout of the General Wayne Inn. Moreover, the three-hundred-year-old stairs of the building creaked loudly when walked on, so it would have been impossible for the killer to surprise their intended victim. All this evidence loudly suggested that Jim Webb had been shot by someone he knew, and a person who had worked in the building long enough to be intimately familiar with it.

Guy Sileo, Jim Webb's business partner, immediately emerged as a prime suspect in the murder. They both had taken out life insurance policies for the sum of $650,000 on one another. This was not uncommon in starting a business, but it raised red flags because Ruby Webb made it known to police that Jim was unhappy in the partnership and had planned to walk away in the new year. What was even more damning was that as Jim's body was being removed from the General Wayne Inn, Guy Sileo approached Ruby Webb, hugged her and said, "Who would have wanted to shoot Jim?" At this time, only the police and the killer knew how Jim died.

Three weeks before Jim Webb was murdered, Guy Sileo purchased a .25-caliber pistol. He turned it over to police, but it was not the murder weapon. Ammunition found in Guy's office did match the bullet that had killed Jim. But Guy Sileo had an alibi for the night that the murder occurred. He had left the General Wayne Inn with twenty-year-old assistant chef Felicia Moyse, with whom the married Guy Sileo was having an affair, to go to a Christmas party, while Jim remained in his office, catching up on paperwork. Felicia and Guy drove to the party in separate cars, with Guy arriving at the party before Felicia because she had to run some errands. This, it seemed, provided Guy Sileo with an alibi for the murder.

Two months later, on February 27, 1997, another tragedy connected with this case occurred. Felicia Moyse took her own life with her father's service revolver, shooting herself in the head. She did not leave a note, but the similarity of her suicide to the murder of Jim Webb did not go unnoticed. Although we can never know for certain, police speculated that Felicia Moyse realized that Guy Sileo had murdered Jim Webb and that he was using her for an alibi even though he was guilty, and she could not continue living with that knowledge. May she rest in peace.

After this second horrific loss of human life, the case went cold for two years. But then employees at the General Wayne Inn remembered that Guy Sileo had once owned a *second* .25-caliber gun that he had never told the police about, a Beretta that was unregistered because Sileo's grandfather had brought it back from fighting in World War II. Guy Sileo denied ever owning such a gun, but when the police convinced an employee at the General Wayne Inn to wear a wire, Sileo was recorded saying he used to own a Beretta but had "gotten rid of it."

The General Wayne Inn in 2011. *Photo by Smallbones. Wikimedia Commons.*

Finally, investigators examined the gun holster provided to them by Guy Sileo, and they found unmistakable marks in the holster indicating it had held a Beretta for many years. Although the actual murder weapon that killed Jim Webb was never found, this forensic evidence was enough to bring Guy Sileo to trial, where he was convicted in 2001 of murdering Jim Webb and sentenced to life imprisonment. As of 2015, Sileo has exhausted his appeals in the court, ensuring that he will likely spend the rest of his life behind bars.

In 2001, after the murder and the subsequent court case, the General Wayne Inn closed for the first time since it opened in 1704 and began to fall into ruin. But in 2005, the General Wayne Inn was reborn. It became the Chabad of the Main Line, a Jewish synagogue and community center, which is still in operation today and regarded as one of the most vibrant Jewish institutions in the state of Pennsylvania.

Regarding the centuries of ghost stories at the General Wayne Inn, Rabbi Shagra Sherman said in an article for the *Philadelphia Inquirer* newspaper in 2005:

> *Whatever negativity transpired in this building, the positivity and holiness that we're going to bring in will marginalize it and push it out the door.... With a mezuzah on every door, the ghosts will be doing their best to be let out of this building…or else we're going to convert them—and count them in the minyan.*

CHAPTER 12

THE MADNESS OF MARY LUM GIRARD

While the City of Philadelphia may honor Stephen Girard, the founder of Girard College, and the primary financier of the War of 1812, not much is known about his wife, Mary Lum Girard.

Who was Mary Lum, and why has her name been undersold in a city that purports to honor its historic figures? A clue can be found on the first floor of Pennsylvania Hospital. A large plaque honoring Stephen Girard's contributions to the hospital also mentions that his wife, Mary Lum, lies buried somewhere near this spot....If Mary Lum is buried somewhere on the grounds of the hospital, where is she, and why isn't her grave noted?

—Thom Nickels, Philadelphia Free Press

Mary Lum was born in Philadelphia in the year 1758. She was the daughter of a shipbuilder and was described by her contemporaries as beautiful, with long, flowing black hair. As was true for many women of her time, any words that Mary herself may have written about her life have not survived. There are no letters or diaries, and no one who knew her ever recorded a single word she said, as far as we know. She has become a mostly forgotten tragic footnote in American history. When Mary Lum is remembered at all, it is chiefly as the wife of Stephen Girard, the millionaire who left an indelible mark upon the city of Philadelphia. Mary Lum is also remembered today for a darker reason: her insanity—and her restless ghost.

Eighteen years old when the Declaration of Independence was signed in 1776, Mary Lum had another reason to cherish that memorable year. In 1776, amid the whirlwind of revolution in Philadelphia, Mary Lum met and fell in love with a newly arrived twenty-six-year-old French grocery store owner named Stephen Girard. In 1777, she married him.

Born in Bordeaux as the son of an ordinary sailor in 1750, Stephen Girard became blind in his right eye when he was eight years old. He arrived in Philadelphia in 1776 and quickly became a successful businessman. Eventually, his fortune became immense. When he died, he was the richest man in the nation. According to a study done in 1996, adjusting for inflation, Stephen Girard was still the fourth-wealthiest person ever to live in the United States of America, behind John D. Rockefeller, Cornelius Vanderbilt and John Jacob Astor.

After their wedding in 1777, Mary Lum and Stephen Girard apparently had a happy married life for eight years. However, in 1785, it began to be whispered among Philadelphia's elite circle that Mary Girard had become insane. She was twenty-seven years old. It is reported that Mary began to become emotionally unstable, often having uncontrollable and sometimes violent outbursts of extreme sadness or of deep rage. Stephen Girard wrote in a letter to his brother: "If it is not a physical ailment, it is of the mind....The illness of this virtuous woman has so so unsettled my life." As Mary's mental illness progressed, Stephen wrote of her "sickness" and her "derangements." Some records say Mary was found walking the streets in her nightgown.

It is not recorded what caused Mary Lum's descent into the private hell of mental illness, but after two years, Stephen Girard had enough of his wife's madness. In 1787, he took a mistress, beginning a sexual relationship with a younger woman named Sally Bickham. Considering his marriage to be effectively over, Stephen Girard then moved Sally Bickham into the house while Mary was still living there. Mary's thoughts and feelings about these events are not known. But it is easy to imagine that being forced to live with her husband's much younger girlfriend would have had a negative effect on Mary's state of mind.

In *The Life and Times of Stephen Girard*, author John Bach McMaster writes of this time:

> *A consultation of eminent physicians was called, who were unanimous in the belief that the sole hope for the restoration of her sanity lay in her immediate removal to a hospital....The only hospital in Philadelphia at*

Engraving of Stephen Girard by
Alonzo Chappel. *Public domain.*

*the time which received such patients was Pennsylvania Hospital, at Eighth
and Spruce Streets.*

On August 31, 1790, Stephen Girard had Mary Lum committed to
Pennsylvania Hospital in Philadelphia as an "incurable lunatic." She was
thirty-two years old and, according to her husband and others, had been
insane for five years at the time of her confinement. The person responsible
for forcibly committing Mary Lum Girard to Pennsylvania Hospital was,
somewhat ironically, none other than Dr. Benjamin Rush, one of the signers
of the Declaration of Independence. Dr. Rush himself described the insane
patients' rooms at Pennsylvania Hospital as "cold and damp in the winter,
hot in the summer, lacking ventilation, stuffy and malodorous."

Mary Lum Girard was assigned a "spacious" room on the first floor of
Pennsylvania Hospital and was permitted to walk the hospital's grounds with
supervision. Unlike most other mental patients at the hospital, Mary was
also allowed to receive visitors with few restrictions. It is unknown if Stephen
Girard ever came to visit her or if anyone ever did.

Shortly after Mary was confined at Pennsylvania Hospital, she gave birth to a baby girl, whom she named after herself. Her child died at five months old, and although we do not know, it is almost certain that the death of her baby plunged her further into grief. Stephen Girard never had any children with his mistresses, suggesting to some he may have been infertile. The father of Mary's child was likely another man. It is possible to imagine that after her husband moved his mistress, Sally Bickham, into the house, Mary may have taken a lover of her own. There are unverified rumors, handed down over time, that the father of Mary Lum's child was Black. For the racist, slave-owning Stephen Girard, it is easy to imagine this would have been the last straw. Perhaps that is the real reason Mary was committed to Pennsylvania Hospital in 1790. We cannot know for sure. But in 1787, Stephen Girard did write these words in a letter to his brother:

Having been so foolish as to marry this unfortunate vixen…I treat her properly but at the same time I despise her as much as it is possible to despise anyone….I hate her like the devil and note with pleasure that this feeling increases from day to day.

Stephen Girard was a rich and powerful man in Philadelphia. No one asked any questions.

Mary Lum Girard never left Pennsylvania Hospital. She remained imprisoned there for twenty-five years before dying on September 15, 1815. Mary Lum Girard was only fifty-six years old when she died. Her cause of death is not recorded.

Stephen Girard ordered that Mary's body be laid to rest on the grounds of Pennsylvania Hospital in an unmarked grave on the northern lawn. A man named Professor William Wagner was present at the funeral for Mary Lum Girard, and he later recalled:

Towards the close of the day, after the sun had withdrawn his last beams from the tallest sycamore which shades the garden, Mr. Girard was sent for, and when he arrived with all his family the plain coffin of Mary Girard was carried forward to her resting place in deepest silence. I shall never forget the last and closing scene. We all stood about the coffin when Mr. Girard, filled with emotion, stepped forward, kissed his wife's corpse, and his tears moistened her cheek….Following a hush of a few minutes' duration, the coffin was lowered into the grave, and another silence ensued, after which Girard bent over and bestowed a last look upon his dead wife,

Pennsylvania Hospital as it appears today. *Photo by Carol M. Highsmith. Courtesy of the Library of Congress.*

then, turning from the new-made grave, said to Samuel Coates, "It is very well," and immediately returned to his home.

This all sounds quite sadly romantic, but it is important to remember the detail Wagner gives in his first sentence. Mary Lum Girard's funeral took place after the sun had set, in darkness, so no passersby could see. She was hidden away from the world to the very end.

WE CANNOT KNOW WHAT Mary thought or felt during the final years of her life. Her lived human experience has been lost to time. Her true voice remains elusive and silent. Or perhaps not entirely silent. From soon after her death up to the present day, stories have circulated throughout Philadelphia of Mary Lum Girard's ghost haunting Pennsylvania Hospital.

Patients housed in the room where she died often reported waking up in the middle of the night to see a strange woman standing at the foot of their bed, staring down at them, before suddenly vanishing. The apparition of a woman in a white dress has been seen walking the grounds of Pennsylvania Hospital, often disappearing on the north lawn, near the site where Mary Lum Girard is buried. No paintings or sketches of Mary have survived, so it is impossible to know for sure if she is the ghost many people have seen. In the vicinity of Mary's old room on the first floor, sounds of a woman crying inconsolably have sometimes been heard. Upon investigation, there is no one there.

What of Stephen Girard himself? He died on December 26, 1831, at the age of eighty-one, sixteen years after the death of Mary. The wealthiest man in the United States at the time of his death, Stephen Girard was buried in the Catholic cemetery of Holy Trinity Church, despite being an atheist all his life. The church was and still is located at Sixth and Spruce Streets, just two blocks away from Mary's unmarked grave at Pennsylvania Hospital.

Twenty years after his burial, the remains of Stephen Girard were exhumed and reinterred in a tomb built in the Founder's Hall vestibule of Girard College across town. Ever since his remains were moved, people passing by the gates of Holy Trinity Church's cemetery at night have been startled to see the figure of an old man standing among the old tombstones, a man who looks down at the ground and then mysteriously vanishes. Does the ghost of Stephen Girard haunt the earth because his bones were moved, or does he remain out of guilt or as a punishment for what he did to his wife, Mary Lum, whose sorrowful ghost haunts the hospital just two blocks away?

ON JULY 4, 1976, Lanie Roberston's powerful one-act play *The Insanity of Mary Girard* premiered in Philadelphia. Concord Theatricals describes the show like this:

> *In 1790, Mary Girard is committed to an asylum. After Mary became pregnant by another man, her husband had her declared legally insane. Now, Mary sits in a chair as the "furies" dance around and impersonate people from her past. By the end of this haunting and highly theatrical piece, she has grown rather convincingly into her diagnosis.*

The play, described by the *Times-Picayune* newspaper as "an engrossing drama on the abuse of the mentally ill," continues to be performed all over the world, raising awareness of Mary Lum Girard's important and harrowing story. One of the most recent productions of *The Insanity of Mary Girard* was an immersive staging at Allens Lane Theater in Philadelphia as part of the 2019 Fringe Festival, directed with imagination and incisive fury by Mariangela Saavedra.

A reporter named Thom Nickels wrote an article for the *Philadelphia Free Press* with the title: "Is Pennsylvania Hospital Hiding the 'Shame' of Mary Girard?" In this article, Nickels recounts meeting three veterans of World War II named Joe Vendetti, Charlie Roseman and Bob Ross; the latter two graduated from Girard College in 1939. Vendetti said:

When these two guys and I would get together they talked about their college days. When I retired in 1973, I took up research about Stephen Girard and I thought, "Oh my God, Stephen Girard's wife has been forgotten and ignored."

It particularly distressed them that her grave remained unmarked. So they pooled their money and had a tombstone made to mark the location of Mary's remains. Finally, Mary Lum Girard would have the memorial she deserved, and perhaps her troubled soul would now cease to walk the hallways and lawns. These men donated the ornate tombstone to Pennsylvania Hospital, and Pennsylvania Hospital refused to accept it. Thom Nickels concludes his article with the words:

A shadow of embarrassment and shame seemed to cover Mary Lum's legacy, proving that the stigma of mental illness, while far worse in the 19th century, still carried considerable weight in modern times.

Perhaps, one day, the grave of Mary Lum Girard will finally be marked, and her spirit will rest in peace. Until then, it is important that the tragic story of her life and her struggle with the demons inside her mind be remembered and not forgotten in the crumbling pages of old histories. Not buried in the darkness but brought back up again, at last, into the light, forever.

THE CITY OF RESTLESS SPIRITS

My friends, I hope you've enjoyed these stories from the *Haunted History of Philadelphia*. There are many more spine-tingling tales of the supernatural side of this great city to be told, too many for only one book. You may not believe in ghosts at all, but even if you do not, I recommend visiting each of these places and taking in the extraordinary history that is all around you, no matter where you turn in Philadelphia. With so much history within these buildings, these streets and our burial grounds, it doesn't take much imagination to think that perhaps some of that history might linger behind, that the spirits of those long dead may remain here, watching us from the shadows. Walk around Old City with the Ghost Tour of Philadelphia once it gets dark, or take a night tour of Eastern State Penitentiary—I guarantee you will feel something, a presence that seems to be all around you. The past coming alive in ways you may not expect.

And then, when you return to your home or hotel room and turn out the lights, don't be surprised if you wake up in the middle of the night to find something in the room that shouldn't be there, something standing in a corner that is darker than the darkness. You might begin to hear footsteps slowly walking toward your bed, making the floorboards creak as the clock strikes midnight. You might feel something staring at you as you try not to look, feeling something breathing very close to your face, something that's been dead for a very long time. You might tell yourself it's only a nightmare,

Christ Church Burial Ground.

and perhaps it is—or perhaps one of the ghosts of Philadelphia has decided to follow you home…and never leave.

Until we meet again in the night, in the dark, I wish you very pleasant dreams. Good night. Sleep tight.

BIBLIOGRAPHY

Adams, Charles J., III. *Montgomery County Ghost Stories*. Reading, PA: Exeter House Books, 2000.

————. *Philadelphia Ghost Stories*. Rev. ed. Reading, PA: Exeter House Books, 2005.

Boudreau, George W. *Independence: A Guide to Historic Philadelphia*. Yardley, PA: Westholme, 2012.

Bracelin, Cynthia. *Philadelphia's Haunted Historic Walking Tour*. Atglen, PA: Schiffer, 2013.

Dickey, Colin. *Ghostland: An American History in Haunted Places*. New York: Penguin Books, 2016.

Green, Jennifer L. *Dark History of Penn's Woods: Murder, Madness, and Misadventure in Southeastern Pennsylvania*. Havertown, PA: Casemate, 2021.

Hoffman, Elizabeth P. *In Search of Ghosts: Haunted Places in the Delaware Valley*. Philadelphia, PA: Camino Books, 1992.

Johnston, Norman. *Eastern State Penitentiary: Crucible of Good Intentions*. Philadelphia, PA: Philadelphia Museum of Art, 1994.

Kahan, Paul. *Eastern State Penitentiary: A History*. Charleston, SC: The History Press, 2008.

Keels, Thomas H. *Wicked Philadelphia: Sin in the City of Brotherly Love*. Charleston, SC: The History Press, 2010.

Lake, Matt. *Weird Pennsylvania*. New York: Sterling, 2005.

Miller, Marla R. *Betsy Ross and the Making of America*. New York: Henry Holt, 2010.

Oordt, Darcy. *Haunted Philadelphia*. Guilford, CT: Rowman and Littlefield, 2015.

Powell, J.H. *Bring Out Your Dead: The Great Plague of Yellow Fever in Philadelphia in 1793*. Mansfield Centre, CT: Martino, 2016.

Reeser, A.L. *Angel of the Odd: Edgar Allan Poe's Last Days in Philadelphia*. Monococy, PA: 1stSight Press, 2009.

Reeser, Tim. *Ghost Stories of Philadelphia, PA*. Monocacy, PA: 1stSight Press, 2007.

Staib, Walter. *The City Tavern Cookbook: Recipes from the Birthplace of American Cuisine*. Philadelphia, PA: Running Press, 2009.

Watson, John F. *Annals of Philadelphia*. Philadelphia, PA: E.L. Carey & A. Hart, 1830.

Weigley, Russell F. *Philadelphia: A 300 Year History*. New York: W.W. Norton, 1982.

White, Thomas. *Witches of Pennsylvania: Occult History and Lore*. Charleston, SC: The History Press, 2013.

About the Author

Josh Hitchens was born and raised in Sussex County, Delaware. He has been a storyteller for the Ghost Tour of Philadelphia since 2007. Josh is also a theater director, actor, playwright and teaching artist who has been called "Philadelphia's foremost purveyor of the macabre" by local press. His first book, *Haunted History of Delaware*, was released in 2021 by Arcadia Publishing. Josh is deeply honored to tell the stories of his second home in *Haunted History of Philadelphia*. He is also the creator of the podcasts *Going Dark Theatre*—which examines the humanity behind the horror in true tales of ghost stories, unsolved mysteries and weird history—as well as *Hitchens on Horror*, in which he acts as a host for some of your favorite scary movies. Josh has also written articles for *Philadelphia Weekly* and the *Broad Street Review*. He lives in West Philadelphia with his partner and a cat named Mina. www.joshhitchens.com.

Visit us at
www.historypress.com